GERMAN HISTORY

An Assessment by German Historians

GERMAN HISTORY
1933-45

An Assessment by German Historians

by

HERMANN MAU and
HELMUT KRAUSNICK

OSWALD WOLFF (PUBLISHERS) LIMITED
London

Translated from the German by
ANDREW and EVA WILSON

© OSWALD WOLFF (PUBLISHERS) LIMITED

FIRST PUBLISHED 1959
REPRINTED 1961, 1962, 1963, 1964, 1968
FIRST PAPERBACK EDITION 1971
REPRINTED 1973, 1978

REPRINTED IN GREAT BRITAIN BY
LEWIS REPRINTS LTD.
MEMBER OF BROWN KNIGHT & TRUSCOTT GROUP
LONDON AND TONBRIDGE

Contents

CONTENTS

Introduction

FEW countries have had their recent history more thoroughly analysed by foreign historians than has Germany, while assessments by German historians, particularly in an English translation, are comparatively rare.

Yet the questions to which one seeks an answer by German historians are many.

How could a nation, stumbling out of the defeat of the First World War, put itself, with every appearance of willingness, into the hands of a Dictator prepared to subject Europe to a new war? How did Hitler win the hearts or votes of forty out of forty-five million Germans in the plebiscite of November 12th 1933? How could the barriers go down before him: the Centre, the Social-Democrats, the Communists, the trade unions—all those elements which one would have expected to offer effective resistance to Nazism?

The answers to these questions, and the many others which follow from them, are intrinsic to a History which begins with the confusions and divisions at the close of the Weimar Republic and ends with the abyss of 1945.

The broad facts of the period are known. What the reader will find new here (apart from a compact and comprehensive summary) is a careful and intimate appraisal of the psychology of the period.

He is taken, for a start, to the spirit of escapism in Germany in the early 'thirties, the blind urge, after wartime defeat and economic crises, to regain self-confidence and unload the burden of responsibility.

Upon this fertile soil falls Nazism, appearing in a variety of poses: the ally of conservative nationalism, the pioneer of a new classless Socialism, even, for a brief, fantastic moment, the self-styled defender of the Christian faith.

Events thereafter—Hitler's establishment with the aid of the Conservatives, the decimation of the leaders of the Left, the mass desertion of the rank and file to the Leader whose credentials they dare not examine—are unfolded from the pen of one who lived through them.* One sees Hitler on the "Day of National Awakening", posed with Hindenburg against the tomb of Frederick the Great at Potsdam; two days later he is proclaiming revolution in the Reichstag, where, having obtained his infamous Enabling Bill, he is able, like the player who holds all the Jokers, to wind up every organ of constitutional opposition.

Before the régime is fully in control, there is Roehm's campaign for a "continuation" of the revolution, and here again the book throws a revealing sidelight on the aura of respectability which descended on Hitler through Roehm's suppression.

From the bloodbath of June 30th 1934 the reader is taken swiftly through the mood of the years which followed, when Nazism ceased to be a "movement" and developed into a

* Hermann Mau, the author of the first part of this book, was born in 1913. He had completed it up to p. 119, when he was killed in a motoring accident. The last three sections were added by H. Krausnick, and the book was part of a work edited by Professor P. Rassow, *Deutsche Geschichte im Ueberblick*, originally published by Metzlersche Verlagsbuchhandlung and C. E. Poeschel, Stuttgart.

rigid system of power and terror. One follows the penetration of every branch of national life by spies and controllers, the rise of Himmler's SS, the methodical extension of the concentration camps, the terrible programmes of "euthanasia" and genocide.

It would be easy for such a book to become an *apologia*, laying the blame for every evil on the Party and the SS; but it does not. Though dwelling on the thoroughness with which the Party stifled every voice of protest, it freely acknowledges the acclaim of the irreligious, a-political mass for Hitler's pre-war diplomatic victories, and later, after an initial setback in Poland, the readiness of the Wehrmacht to turn a blind eye to the atrocities of the terror formations in the occupied territories.

The military events of the Second World War (in contrast to the international events which preceded it) are dealt with cursorily, for the latter part of the book is largely given over to the rise and character of the German "resistance".

Here the "psychological" aspect comes into its own again. We are shown how scattered and amorphous the Resistance was—not a "single movement" but a "variety of overlapping groups". We are given an insight into the conflict of duty with which so many of its members were confronted (and so, by implication, into one reason for the delay before resistance became manifest): the Christian is faced with the necessity to murder, the officer with the necessity of violating his oath of loyalty, the patriot with the risk of seeming to betray his country at a time of ever increasing danger from the East.

To the English reader, secure in his memory of a war which seemed to present no comparable conflict for himself, some of these doubts and hesitations might cause impatience. And justly so, had they not been resolved into action. Yet the fact is that they *were* so resolved, not only in the plot against Hitler of July 20th 1944, but, as we now know, in countless other attempts, equally brave and hazardous, which failed in secret.

England has not always been blameless of refusing its hand to German liberalism, or quick to see through the clichés which have obscured the interplay of forces in Germany more richly than those of any other country. Perhaps this book, by its sincere, brief and readable analysis, will help to blow away some cobwebs. Perhaps, too, it will serve as a reminder that after a decade of Nazism there were Germans who were ready to repair German honour with their lives.

A. W.

1933
THE SEIZURE OF POWER

The End of the Interregnum

BORN in the confusion of an improvised revolution burdened with the inheritance of a lost world war, harassed by incalculable obligations under a severe peace treaty, and weakened by a desperate struggle against economic and social misery, the Weimar Republic, having failed to bring its opponents under control, at last yielded them the field almost without a struggle.

It had hardly ever been faced with a genuine Opposition; only—or almost only—with fanatical enemies. An Opposition keeps within the framework of the existing State, which it recognises as a contractual foundation. In Germany the collapse of 1918 had destroyed the possibility of finding a common basis for the settlement of political differences. The enemies of the Republic refused to accept the State as such from the outset. They professed to stand outside it, while enjoying every advantage conferred on an Opposition by a democratic constitution. Thus it was possible for the State to fall into the hands of its enemies by "legal" means.

When cornered by fate, people tend to seek an object on which to shift the burden of responsibility. The Weimar Republic was just such an object for all who had suffered by reason of the German collapse in 1918, and who baulked at accepting military defeat and the failure of the old order as a fact of history and their ordained lot. For them, the Republic

13

became the cause of every evil, real or imaginary, and they developed the idea that it was only an interregnum, which had to be endured until the way was cleared for a return to the old order.

The idea received a strong impetus from the militant nationalism with which wounded patriotic pride reacted against defeat and revolution. The Republic became the hated obstacle to restoring Germany's power and greatness. Thus, and thus only, there grew up a common political consciousness among its middle-class enemies. The Republic, which permitted itself only very moderate nationalist sentiments, underrated the force of this newly awakened nationalism and delayed too long in directing it into legal channels. By fighting it, it made it strong. Nor could it prevent this nationalism from propagating the idea of the "interregnum" with growing success, and so awakening a popular desire for a fundamental political change.

This development was further encouraged by the fact that the Weimar Republic contained, in the Reichswehr, an important element which was more than tolerant of these ideas. Officially the Reichswehr was the loyal servant of the Republic. It always maintained that it was non-political. But this was due to tactical considerations and not to an effort at genuine loyalty. For, as Blomberg frankly admitted in June 1933, "being non-political never meant that we approved of the system of the earlier governments. It was a way of protecting ourselves against over-involvement in this system". Furthermore, the attitude of the Reichswehr was not non-political, but "above party", and therefore highly political. For when the time came, its position above the parties enabled it to throw its weight into the balance of domestic decisions. The nationalist enemies of the Republic always assumed that in the end the Reichswehr would act in their favour. They were not mistaken.

The nationalists' hope of bringing down the Republic were encouraged, unwittingly, by its second President. It is true that Hindenburg considered himself bound with religious solemnity by the oath he had sworn to uphold the Weimar constitution. But at heart he remained a convinced royalist, and his dream of Germany's future was the restoration of the Hohenzollerns. As a Field-Marshal of Imperial Germany, Hindenburg actually personified the very ideas in whose name the nationalists opposed the State of which he was legitimate head. This inner contradiction, which burdened the Republic after 1925, played an important part in the development of the nation's political consciousness, not towards democracy, but away from it. Hindenburg was not a democratic prototype. As a man, he was always more acceptable to the Republic's enemies than to its defenders.

In the end, it was their readiness—partly secret, partly open —to put an end to the Weimar "interregnum", which united the President, the Reichswehr and the "national opposition" in spite of their antagonism, and which made it possible for Hitler to become Chancellor.

The "National Awakening"

HITLER'S assumption of the chancellorship of the Reich on January 30th 1933 took place within the correct forms prescribed by the constitution. His cabinet was a coalition, in which he himself represented the strongest party in the Reichstag. The share of the Nazis, or to give them their full title, the National Socialist German Workers' Party, in the newly formed Government looked modest enough. Besides Hitler himself, there were only two others: Frick as Minister of the Interior, and Goering as Minister without portfolio and Minister of Aviation. On March 11th they were joined by Goebbels in the newly created office of Minister of Propaganda. The other partner in the coalition, the German National People's Party, was represented by its chairman, Hugenberg, who took over the Ministries of Economic Affairs and of Food and Agriculture, and by the Minister of Justice, Guertner. The remaining members of the cabinet, the Vice-Chancellor von Papen, the Defence Minister von Blomberg, the Minister of Labour Seldte, as well as the ministers taken over from the Schleicher Cabinet—von Neurath (Foreign Affairs), Count Schwerin von Krosigk (Finance) and Eltz von Ruebenach (Post and Communications)—were right-wing Independents, considered closer to the Nationalists than to the Nazis.

In this way, Hitler's appointment as Chancellor appeared to

the German public not so much a victory for the Nazis as a victory for the "national opposition" in general. True, the earlier cabinets of Papen and Schleicher had already been cabinets of the "national opposition" in which the constitutionalist parties no longer had a share. But they had still been obliged to contend with violent Nazi opposition. They had represented only a part of those nationalist forces which now, under Hitler's chancellorship, formed a firm front for the first time. With this, the Republic was delivered into the control of men who held at least one conviction in common: that the Republic had become bankrupt and must be wound up.

Although, outwardly, the change of Government had been made within the framework of the law, the public was quick to notice that something revolutionary had happened. A sudden change of attitudes became apparent. People who had never been willing to identify themselves with any Government of the Republic now put their confidence in the new one; and those who hitherto had supported the State now felt menaced by it. It was this process which people—not yet appreciating what had happened—called the "Umbruch" (break-up).

Hitler himself provided the public with the catchword that summed up events since January 30th. In a "Proclamation to the German People" on February 1st, he first used the phrase "national awakening". At the same time he established the pattern on which the masses were taught to think. The change of Government was represented as a decisive break with the now almost proverbial "fourteen years" of shameful past, leading to the "reconstruction" and "rise" of the German nation.

B

17

"National awakening" was the picture on the drop-curtain temporarily to be lowered on the diverse scene of events. It was a picture which the many differing forces supporting the new Government could accept without difficulty. It symbolised the end of the interregnum of the "fourteen years", it did justice to the emotional fervour with which this end was hailed by part of the masses, and it was vague enough to avoid committing any of the participants in advance.

The central figure in this picture was not Hitler, but Hindenburg. How ambiguous a figure he was now became manifest. One moment he was the guardian of the Weimar Constitution, the old gentleman in the plain frock-coat; the next he was back as the wartime Field-Marshal in the order-bedecked uniform of Imperial Germany. We can discern the re-transformation not only in the phrasing of his official pronouncements at the time, but also in a significant action: on March 15th, as constitutional Supreme Commander of the Reichswehr, he authorised it to wear the black, white and red cap button, "thereby manifesting the close bond between the German armed forces and the resurgent national vigour of the German people".

Hitler was at pains to conform with this mood. His first official pronouncement as Chancellor followed the pattern of those time-hallowed generalisations which gained popular currency now that the "fourteen years" had been mentally excluded in a kind of parenthesis. At this time, too, he liked to affect Christian convictions. In his proclamation of February 1st he gave an assurance that his Government would "firmly protect Christianity, which is our moral basis"; and he concluded with the words: "May Almighty God show mercy on our work, guide our will, bless our understanding, and favour us with the confidence of our people." On February 11th, in the Berlin Sportpalast, Papen spoke of the "new Christian Reich of the German nation". Whole SA (Brownshirt) formations went to church. In the *Voelkischer Beobachter*, the official organ of the Nazi Party, there appeared a leading article headed: "Christianity: the basis of Adolf Hitler's Government".

All this was crowned by a "Day of National Awakening" (March 21st) when President, Government and Reichstag assembled at the tomb of Frederick the Great in the Garrison Church at Potsdam and presented the world with the spectacle of German bourgeois nationalism celebrating its victory. There was a picture which became for many Germans the symbol of a new era: Hindenburg, in the uniform (and pose) of an Imperial Field-Marshal, shaking hands with a reverently bowing Hitler before the Garrison Church porch.

But this amiable picture, however reassuring to so many who went in fear of this new and unknown force, was an illusion. The whole picture of the "national awakening" bore no relation to political reality. It was an exaggerated gloss, a playing-up of the part of conservative German nationalism in the events of January 30th, an attempt—which seemed to recommend itself to the Nazi leaders for tactical reasons—to make things look harmless by a planned propaganda campaign.

The Nazis' view of things was very different, and this was what counted. For Hitler the chancellorship meant the power he had so feverishly craved since the early twenties, when he adopted the role of "Fuehrer" in Munich. The "seizure of power" was the target on which for years he had trained his party. It was the prelude to realising his political programme: after the "struggle" the long-prophesied "victory". Hitler had never left any doubt that this victory would be his alone, solely and indivisibly; that the Nazis would claim complete power, and that he would demand for himself the same position of leadership which he had gained in his own party.

But Hitler had good reasons for not bringing this aspect into prominence at the outset. The circumstances of his coming to power obliged him to make concessions. The political grouping to which he owed his chancellorship was founded on the expectation that he would wield his power as a loyal partner of those who had helped him into the saddle. It was in his interest to retain others' faith in his loyalty as long as possible. Therefore it was not unwelcome that all the parties, unions and groups which had rallied behind his Government should believe it was they who had achieved the victory on January 30th, and that there should arise a wave of nationalist emotions which could easily be made into the "national awakening".

This, then, is the starting-point of a complete split of reality by propaganda, which from now on characterises the structure of political events. What actually happens, and the picture the public receives through the medium of propaganda, become two different things. The events immediately following January 30th must already be seen in this light. For propaganda at once set to work to lay a smoke-screen over the fact that the Nazi leaders—in spite of all their assurances of loyalty to their political partners—were making directly for complete and sole possession of power.

The Reichstag Fire and the Enabling Bill

ONE of the arguments used to quieten Hindenburg's stubborn resistance to Hitler's nomination had been that a coalition cabinet of Nazis and German Nationalists would mean, after two years of presidential government, a return to the normal constitutional form of parliamentary government. On November 6th 1932 the coalition parties disposed of barely 42 per cent of the votes in the Reichstag. Although not a majority, this was much more than the presidential governments of Papen and Schleicher had ever possessed. Furthermore it did not seem impossible that the parliamentary basis of Hitler's Government might be enlarged.

Of course, this Government of notorious anti-parliamentarians had no intention of returning to a parliamentary form of government for good. But there was, particularly for Hindenburg's "democratic conscience", a difference in whether the special powers which Hitler's Government demanded were once again derived from the Reich President, or whether they were granted by parliament in a regular vote. Hitler had long decided that his first demand as Chancellor would be for an Enabling Bill. In Hindenburg's eyes it may have weighed in his favour that he meant to achieve this by parliamentary means. After Papen's resignation in November 1932, Hitler had already told the President: "I think I would find a basis on which I and the new Government would get the Reichstag to pass an Enabling Bill. Nobody but myself will ever get these powers from the Reichstag!"

To strengthen the position of his party Hitler had demanded a dissolution. The Nazis expected to increase their vote considerably in an election campaign fought with their newly won powers. Hitler had carried this demand against the objections of Hugenberg, whose party could expect nothing from a new election, even before the cabinet was sworn in on January 30th. Since the President could dissolve the Reichstag only if the Government had been shown incapable of achieving a working majority, Hitler made a pretence of conducting negotiations with the Zentrum. After Hitler had declared them fruitless, Hindenburg dissolved the Reichstag on February 1st. To allay any suspicion that he was by-passing parliament and granting Hitler what he had just refused Schleicher, he fixed the new elections on the earliest possible date, March 5th.

The election campaign was conducted in the atmosphere of latent civil war which had hung over Germany for months. Throughout the country the militant formations of the nationalists went into action. In the van was the Nazi SA, whose terrorist activity showed much more plainly than the attitude of their leaders the nature of the forces which had now entered the arena. On the opposing side the most active element was the Communists; no less militant than the SA, they were now more unscrupulous in their methods than ever, since everything was at stake for them. The Nazis' propaganda, however, was master in the field. They used it in accordance with their long experience that the masses were

22

never more easily swayed than when their attention was focused on a dangerous enemy. From the first this propaganda was sharply anti-Communist and gained emphasis from bloodshed in the streets.

One week before the election, on the evening of February 27th, the Reichstag building caught fire. The fire was deliberate. But only the tool of the incendiaries was caught, the half-crazed young Dutchman van der Lubbe, a notorious pyromaniac. The Nazi leaders reacted with a speed and precision compatible with their having expected the event. The same night, the blame was officially laid on the Communists. Four thousand Communist functionaries were arrested, the Communist Press banned, and the situation further made use of to place a temporary ban on the Social Democrat Press as well.

The Communists accused of arson were later acquitted by the Supreme Court for lack of evidence. Van der Lubbe was sentenced to death and executed. He never betrayed his Nazi masters, and it is still an open question whether the latter acted on orders from their leaders or on their own; i.e. whether Hitler was waiting for the fire as a pretext for initiating his long-planned action against the Communist Party, or whether it came as a welcome surprise to him.

The short-term tactical aim of this action was concerned with the election. The Communists were eliminated from the campaign, and the Social Democrats, already handicapped by illegal local measures in the constituencies, lost their Press for the last week of it. But to the German people, who to begin with could not perceive what had really happened, the terrifying picture of the burning Reichstag confirmed the

Nazi prognosis of Bolshevik chaos and decided many to vote for the Nazi Party with its ardent claims to be the saviour from disaster.

At the same time, without the general public foreseeing the consequences, the Reichstag fire was made the excuse for a measure directed far beyond its pretext—defence against Communist violence. On February 28th the President issued a special edict for "Protection of State and People", counter-signed by Hitler, Frick and Guertner, which revoked the constitutional guarantees of personal freedom. This special edict sealed the fate of the Weimar Republic. It gave Hitler powers which within a few months enabled him to eliminate his enemies, get the better of his coalition partners, and secure his party's autocracy. Hindenburg may well have stilled his conscience with the thought that his predecessor, Ebert, had also occasionally revoked the guarantees of fundamental rights. But he seems not to have realised that the edict he was signing lacked a clause contained in all similar edicts of his predecessor, preventing arbitrary action. This clause guaranteed any detained person the right to a hearing before a court within twenty-four hours, the right to legal assistance, and the right to protest to a higher court with authority to cancel the arrest.

Against arbitrary enforcement of the edict of February 28th there were no safeguards whatsoever. The police were now able to make arrests without warrant or juridical control, to detain persons for an unlimited period, to search houses, open private letters, ban or censor newspapers, dissolve parties and associations, forbid meetings, and confiscate private property. The power was Hitler's, since the police were under control of

Frick as Minister of the Interior, and of Goering as Minister of the Interior of the largest Land, Prussia. The edict remained in force until the end of the Nazi régime.

The elections of March 5th procured a narrow majority for the Government parties. The German Nationalist Party, with fifty-two seats, neither lost nor gained. The Nazis, who had used their power and influence ruthlessly during the campaign, increased their representation from 196 to 288. This gave the Government parties 340 out of 647 seats in the new Reichstag. The increased votes came from Communists, former non-voters, and young people voting for the first time. On March 5th nearly four million more people went to the polls than at the previous elections in November 1932, and there were only small changes in the votes of the other parties. Thus the Social Democrats kept 120 of their 121 seats, and the Bavarian People's Party nineteen of their twenty, while the Zentrum raised its representation from seventy to seventy-three. The Communists lost nineteen seats of their former 100. Even so, 4·8 million people voted for them, although it was already certain that the Communist deputies would be unable to take their seats. They were under arrest, and remained so, except for those who had gone abroad or underground.

Both Government parties had declared before polling day that the elections on March 5th were to be the last. The newly elected Reichstag had but one purpose: to pass an Enabling Bill eliminating parliament and giving the Government a completely free hand. Such a Bill meant a change in the constitution and required a two-thirds majority. After eliminating the Communists, Hitler still needed thirty-one votes for this. There were several ways of getting them. Thanks to the edict of February 28th, he could arrest Opposition deputies. On the day of the decisive vote, nine Social Democrat deputies were under arrest; and the threat hung over the assembly that arrests would continue during the Bill's three readings until the two-thirds majority was secured. Another way was offered by disagreements among the bourgeois parties of the centre. There were quite a few deputies who sympathised with the Nazis and, as the Nazis well knew, had threatened to vote against their own parties if they should turn the Bill down. Finally, if Hitler could win over the strongest centre party, the Zentrum, the remaining ones could be expected to adopt the Zentrum's lead. To the last moment Hitler kept all three possibilities open, and in the end chose the third.

In considering the pros and cons, the parties of the centre were under the impression that they would be unable to prevent the passage of the Bill and that, even if they delayed it, nothing could stop Hitler deriving powers from the edict of February 28th, which already went further than the Bill. By agreeing to the Enabling Bill they could perhaps obtain the repeal of the dangerous edict. Was not the main thing to prevent Hitler using the edict to dissolve Opposition parties? Was it not essential to keep these intact in case the President, as was hoped, should change his mind and put a stop to the proceedings? And finally, would not Hitler seize by force what parliament refused him, and would it not be more politic to accept the Enabling Bill as a means of keeping him within the law?

These considerations caused the Zentrum to assent to the Bill, on condition that Hitler agreed to restore the basic rights which had been suspended by the edict. Hitler gave his verbal agreement to these conditions and promised to put it in writing in a letter to the Zentrum. This letter, however, had not yet been received when the decisive Reichstag session of March 23rd began. Only after Frick had assured the chairman of the Zentrum, Kaas, that the letter was already on its way, did the Zentrum decide to give its support. So the Bill was passed by 441 votes against those of the ninety-four Social Democrat deputies present. This would have represented the necessary two-thirds majority, even if the absent Social Democrat and Communist deputies had been able to vote. The Zentrum waited for Hitler's letter in vain. In fact he never wrote it, and the edict was never repealed.

In a speech of great courage and dignity, Wels, the chairman of the Social Democrats, gave his party's reasons for rejecting the Enabling Bill. He was answered by Hitler with derision and malevolent triumph. It was the Reichstag's last debate. By assenting to the Enabling Bill parliament had put itself out of action.

The National Emergency Termination Bill, as the Enabling Bill was officially called, gave the Government four years' power to enact laws without parliamentary sanction, explicitly including even laws which might deviate from the constitution. To make it more palatable, some restrictions were incorporated which could be regarded as safeguards against its abuse. Thus no law might be enacted on the strength of the Bill which affected the Reichstag or the upper house, the Reichsrat, or interfered with the rights of the Reich President. Furthermore its powers were conferred not upon Hitler but upon the Government as a whole, so that it would lapse automatically if the Hitler Government were superseded before the end of the Bill's validity. But in the event these restrictions never stopped Hitler from completely transforming the State according to his own ideas, and from finally overriding the very rights which the Enabling Bill was meant to preserve.

1933-4
THE NAZI REVOLUTION

The End of the Parties

ON March 21st, against a heroic, conservative backcloth of black, white and red at the Garrison Church in Potsdam, Hitler had once again evoked the picture of a "national awakening" and talked of the "great task of reorganising the German people". Two days later, and certain of the Enabling Bill, he addressed the Reichstag in the Kroll Opera House in Berlin, which had been turned into a temporary Chamber. Now he used a markedly changed tone and spoke openly of "revolution". This did not happen by accident. It was purely out of tactical considerations that the Nazi leadership had so far exercised official restraint and encouraged among its bourgeois allies and fellow travellers the optimistic illusion that Nazi exuberance could be controlled and contained within their own more harmless sense of a "national awakening". Hitler's open avowal of revolution was a declaration that the Nazi leadership, having achieved its tactical purpose with the Enabling Bill, no longer felt bound by these considerations. The revolution took its course.

Who was to resist it? The two potential centres of resistance from Weimar days, the Socialist bastion of the workers and the nationalist bastion of the middle classes, collapsed under the assault of the revolutionary forces. Nazi propaganda had long sown doubts and uncertainty among both groups' supporters by promising that National Socialism would end the political and social strife of the past. When Hitler abolished their political organisations, nothing remained. In the end the great desertion to the victorious revolution left the functionaries standing alone.

Among the parties of the Weimar system it was only the Social Democrats who had maintained unequivocal and uncompromising opposition to the Nazis. Communist opposition was devalued by its having been neither of these things during the years of the Nazis' rise to power. Admittedly Communists and Nazis fought each other with the hatred of feuding brothers; but this did not prevent them from occasionally joining forces in order to jeopardise the working of the Reichstag, which both despised, or to compromise the policy of the Reich Government, which both hated. This cynical collaboration contributed vitally to the failure of parliamentary democracy in the Weimar Republic, which in turn helped the Nazis' rise to power. For the rest, even the most determined enemies of Nazism were unable to accept Communism as an alternative. In view of the general rejection of the aims and methods of German Communism, orientated as they were by the example of the Soviet Union, Hitler could already risk the forcible suppression of the Communist Party in his first weeks of office. Even outside the Nazi camp this measure was regarded as necessary and justified. But similar action against the Social Democrats was something he dared not attempt until the phase of open revolution. By confusing the fundamental differences between Socialists and Communists in the public mind, and by using the anti-Communist aspect of the revolution with its claim to be a struggle against

Marxism, he sent the Social Democrats the way of the Communists on June 22nd.

If the elimination of the workers' parties had required naked force, the end of the bourgeois parties was undramatic. They yielded to the revolution without a fight and resignedly proclaimed their own dissolution. "In full agreement with the Chancellor," as they put it in a declaration of June 27th, "and in recognition of the fact that the Party State has been superseded", the German Nationalist partners in Hitler's coalition set an example of self-dissolution which was followed by the German State Party (June 28th), the Bavarian People's Party (July 4th) and the Zentrum (July 5th).

On July 14th 1933, the Nazi Party was declared by law to be the only political party in Germany, and any attempt to preserve organised membership of the dissolved parties, or to form new ones, was made a criminal offence.

C

"Co-ordination"

THE Nazi Party required its members to show absolute obedience to the decisions of the Party leadership and, ultimately, to the Fuehrer. Initiative within the Party flowed in one direction only: from the leadership, whose decisions were absolute, down to the blindly trusting mass of the rank and file. The idea of Leader and Followers was an attempt to preserve a human relationship within a party organisation which had already hardened in its early stages into a centralised power machine. It was the aim of the revolution that Nazi leadership and Nazi principles of party organisation should impregnate the political life of the whole country. In the jargon of the Nazi power technicians, this process was called "co-ordination".

Under the banner of "co-ordination" the Nazis removed everything which stood in the way of centralising the power of the Reich Government; i.e. they dismantled the federal structure of Germany. This gradual process began with the dispatch of Reich Commissioners to those Laender where parliamentary majorities were keeping the Nazis out of office. Next, under authority from the Enabling Bill, the Reich Government enacted two laws "for the co-ordination of Laender and Reich" (March 31st and April 7th). Under these laws the Land parliaments were re-formed, without new elections, in conformity with the Reichstag election results of

March 5th. The special Reich Commissioners to the Laender became permanent "Reichsstatthalter" controlling their entire administration. In this way the Laender passed under National Socialism, and the decisive influence of the Reich in Land affairs was ensured at the same time. Finally, on January 30th 1934, a law "for the reorganisation of the Reich" degraded the Laender to secondary administrative departments of the Reich by dissolving their parliaments and absorbing their sovereign rights. The ultimate step in transforming the Reich into a centralised unitary state was taken on February 14th 1934 with the dissolution of the Reichsrat, in which the federal character of the Reich had so far been embodied.

That the motive for these measures was a need for power, and not the desire for a balanced, impersonal and permanent constitutional order, was shown by the Prussian variant of the "co-ordination" of Reich and Laender. A start was made with amalgamating the Prussian ministries with the corresponding Reich ministries. But this justifiable reform, which had been planned in Weimar days, was not continued. The needs of the men in power were satisfied by an arrangement whereby Prussia retained her own Finance Ministry and, in deference to Goering, her own Minister President. Similarly, the standardisation of governmental forms, which would have been a logical consequence of the co-ordination, was only carried through where it was in the immediate interest of power: Justice and Police were centralised by the Reich, and thus became highly effective tools in the hands of the Party leadership.

Parallel with the co-ordination of Reich and Laender went the co-ordination of the State and Party. A law "for the reconstitution of the permanent Civil Service", enacted on April 7th 1933, had provided the necessary conditions as far as personnel policy was concerned. In grotesque contrast to its official name, the law provided a means of replacing trouble-some civil servants by reliable party functionaries. The exclusive position of the Party, which was the starting-point of the co-ordination process, had been officially recognised by the law of July 14th forbidding the formation of any other party. This was confirmed in a Basic Law "for the protection of the unity of Party and State" on December 1st 1933. The new law proclaimed that thanks to the "victory of the National Socialist revolution" the Nazi Party was the "supporter of the German state-idea" and was "indissolubly linked with the State". It also promoted the chiefs of the political and military organisations of the National Socialist movement—the "Fuehrer's deputy" (Hess) and the "Chief of Staff of the SA" (Roehm)—to be members of the Reich Government.

But the revolution did not stop short at the co-ordination of the State. Since it expounded not merely an absolutist political programme, but an absolutist ideology as well, its co-ordination measures were directed towards all aspects of German life. In the end not a single sphere escaped its grip. The pattern of party organisation, embracing political, social and cultural life down to its smallest branches, became a model for the uniform pattern which was now imposed upon the whole of German life. With the hierarchy of its functionaries, from Gauleiter down to street-block leader, the Party aimed at nothing less than omnipresence, the penetration of every cell and organ of influence, in an attempt to impose "co-ordination" even on the thoughts of the individual.

Nazism and the German People

THE Nazi revolution changed the face of Germany completely. Within a few months it transformed the Weimar democracy into a party dictatorship, and nothing could stop it from evolving a complete totalitarian power apparatus. It never met effective resistance. Its pretensions were in marked contrast to the ease with which it achieved its successes—successes due only in part to the use of naked force. True, the revolution had been accompanied by terror and violence, costing the lives of hundreds of its opponents and depriving thousands of their freedom or homeland. But as yet this was mainly due to local excesses, which the leadership tolerated rather than organised from above. Violence and terror had not yet been forged into the system of legalised inhumanity which safeguarded the stability of Nazi rule later on. The enormous number of desertions from the ranks of one-time opponents could no more have been brought about by force than could the approval of the masses to the revolution's more successful accomplishments. However one explains the results of the plebiscites of November 12th 1933 (after Germany's withdrawal from the League of Nations) and of August 19th 1934 (after the amalgamation of the presidency and chancellorship in Hitler's own person), they were not—as were later voting figures—systematically falsified. Of those entitled to vote, 88 per cent on the first occasion, and 84 per cent on the second, voted for Hitler and his régime. Rarely had a people followed the banners of a revolution more willingly.

What made the German people so willing to enter into the Nazi adventure, when the portents of disaster were discernible from the start? All reflections on this question lead back to 1918, the decisive year of latter-day German history. For in the shadow of its decisions National Socialism was born.

The epoch-making event of 1918 was the collapse of the German monarchy. To a people which from its earliest memories had known nothing but the monarchic order, this collapse was a shock which affected the deepest layers of consciousness. Only a few were prepared for it and could understand that the end of the monarchy was the inevitable consequence of historical social changes. The mass of the people endured the collapse of the traditional order as an unforeseeable calamity. When it came to sharing responsibility in the creation of a new order they were helpless, for the Republic, which as a matter of principle rejected the hierarchic graduation of political and social claims, denied the existence of inherited authority, which had been one of the basic elements of the old order.

Institutions are outlived by their memory. Long after losing its monarchic institutions a nation may continue to live in the world of ideas associated with them. The process of adjustment to a new order is a slow and difficult process. It is furthermore hampered by man's tendency to ignore reality by clinging to past habits of thought, or by looking forward impatiently to some vague tomorrow. It was in such an atmosphere of escapism that National Socialism developed.

Since 1918 the German people had been undergoing an uneasy process of adjustment. The reactions set up grew more and more violent as the burden of misery laid upon the new order by the aftermath of war increased. One reason for the success of Nazism was that it could express this uneasiness so effectively. Its main attraction was the firmness with which it disavowed the given state of affairs by ignoring the three primary causes of Germany's situation after 1918: that she had lost the war, that she had signed the Treaty of Versailles, and that she had accepted the status of a democratic republic. The development of the Nazi Party reflects the course of the nation's crises and disputes over its new situation. The Party was born during the first five years of the Republic, at the time of the first uneasy reactions to the revolution of 1918. During the apparent tranquillity of the second five years it led a shadowy existence and was hardly noticed. Its impetuous rise began only with the economic crisis, whose catastrophic effect on the country gave birth to a new wave of uneasiness, which in turn led directly to the Nazi revolution.

The programme which proved so irresistible relied more on the radical questions it posed than the answers it provided. Some of the questions seemed to indicate a clearer appreciation of the problems of the time and the underlying distress of the people than did other programmes. The mere satisfaction of having their needs and anxieties understood was sufficient to lead many people to put their trust in Nazism without any wish to analyse the soundness of its programme as to facts. Extreme nationalism was accepted as a cure for the disease which had befallen German self-confidence, though this disease was not merely a reaction to the unhappy outcome of the war but also indicated the incipient disintegration of a "national" way of thinking. Yet nobody asked if this national-ism could be justified on moral or political grounds (though admittedly the terrible significance it was later to assume in connection with Nazi racial theories could not have been foreseen). The Party's professed socialism seemed to many people, and particularly the middle classes, to offer a hope of fulfilling—in a more peaceful manner than Marxism taught—the demands of the working-class movement, whose justice was acknowledged by their own bad conscience. But again nobody observed that the Nazi theoreticians had only a very hazy idea of this "national socialism", and that they were content to meet a vague emotion—which Gregor Strasser once called "the great anti-capitalist longing"—with an equally vague answer. When the Nazis called for a "Volksgemein-schaft" (community of the people), they were putting their finger on a particularly sensitive spot—the distress and loneli-ness of the individual in a society split by class war and petrify-ing in its materialist relationships. The idea of the "Volks-gemeinschaft" aroused much genuine longing. Nobody suspected that there lurked behind it the bleak totalitarian ideal of an amorphous mass without a will of its own.

The Nazis preached the principle of leadership in contrast to the democratic idea of individual responsibility to the common weal. In this they complied with a powerful tendency of the period, which demonstrated clearly the survival of the ideas of the monarchic past. The revolution had disposed of hereditary authority. But it had put in its place nothing to which the people, bound by their habits of thought and living, could offer that trust by which authority is established. The secret of Hitler's rise to dictatorship was his quickness to divine this and to apply the demand for a "leader", which already existed, to himself. With immense success he discovered the people's need and attached to himself the limitless confidence they were prepared to bestow on whoever would promise to relieve them of their burden of responsibility.

The principle of leadership was but one aspect of the Nazi programme which gave it that vivid simplicity responsible for so much of its success. In an age when political realities have become too complicated for the individual to grasp, simplified programmes exert a great attraction. Nazism's crude simplifications made the world seem intelligible again. It provided simple yardsticks for good and bad, value and uselessness, black and white—the things about which people wanted reassurance. Their readiness to accept an illusion in place of reality was proportionate to their perplexity in a world where their inherited set of values no longer sufficed.

But the distressing result of it all remains incomprehensible until one remembers that Nazism surrounded itself with an atmosphere of anti-rational fervour, the unique climate of a "movement", the stimulant of a dynamism without goal or purpose. By paths remote from reason and reflection it spread like a plague, until very nearly a whole nation was ready to break free of its difficulties and embark on a limitless adventure.

The first phase of the Nazi revolution was readily supported by the majority of the German people. The second, which began about the turn of the year 1933-4, betrayed the first signs of disenchantment. But it was only as a result of the bloody winding-up of the revolution on June 30th 1934 that the exuberance supporting the revolution began to cool. As far as the further course of events was concerned, this was unimportant. For during the revolution the Nazi leaders had gained a firm hold on the dynamism of the "movement" which had initially carried them forward. They had learnt the art of directing popular emotions and of giving help in those places where spontaneity languished.

The "Second Revolution"

BEFORE the revolution was many months old it became clear that Hitler was unable to master the forces he had released. Addressing the SA leaders (on July 1st) and the Reichsstatthalter (on July 6th) he declared that the revolution had reached its conclusion. In a decree of July 11th summing up these declarations, Frick, the Minister of the Interior, gave a hint of some forms of revolutionary activity by his own men which were starting to worry Hitler: disregard of State authority and, worse still, attempts to undermine it; assumption of governmental powers by "this and that organisation or party department"; unauthorised interference in the economy. The decree made it clear that it was a matter not of discipline but of policy. Hitler declared that "the liberated stream of the revolution must now be guided into the safe channel of evolution". But there were forces at work which, in the words of Frick's decree, were contemplating a "continuation of the revolution" or a "second revolution". The transition to the period of evolution was thus "gravely endangered".

Here the deep-seated differences of opinion existing within the Nazi leadership about the nature and the aim of the revolution became apparent for the first time. At first Hitler's appeals to end the revolution seemed successful. There was a period of relaxation, and at the end of 1933 many people told

43

themselves hopefully that life in Germany would resume its normal course. But beneath the surface the fire continued to smoulder. From the spring of 1934 onwards, the "second revolution" was again being talked about. The tensions within the Nazi leadership reached dangerous proportions. Finally it became manifest to all the world that it was split from top to bottom. On June 30th 1934 Hitler dealt with the rift in his own fashion.

The murders of June 30th are cloaked with an almost impenetrable mystery to this day. There is hardly another event of the Nazi epoch whose traces have been so painstakingly effaced. Those chiefly responsible are no longer alive. The essential facts can be reconstructed, but in many particulars we are obliged to rely on circumstantial evidence, since there are scarcely any surviving documents.

Between the civil organisation of the Party and the SA, so different in sociological structure, there had long been latent antagonism. Constructed on military lines by the former Reichswehr captain Ernst Roehm, the SA had rendered Hitler invaluable service as a weapon in his struggle for power. It had been the "anti-terror" instrument against rival organisations during the street battles. But when power had been achieved and the days of church-going and torchlight processions were over, a question arose for which nobody was prepared: what was one to do with the Brownshirts now? The SA regarded itself, not without justification, as the real victor. But the expected reward never came. Hitler had no use for the SA except as the revolution's auxiliary police. In August 1933 Goering dissolved it as such, and Roehm, its Chief of Staff, was left high and dry. It should not be assumed that his disinheritance was Hitler's intention; Roehm's reputation as a notorious homosexual was at this stage no argument against him in Hitler's eyes, nor had it been so before. But the only post which really interested Roehm—the Ministry of Defence —was still beyond the Nazis' grasp. The conversion of the police, in which the SA had secured a few district commissionerships, into a SA stronghold was frustrated by Goering, who as Prussian Minister of the Interior had a stronger pull in this matter.

In this situation, the SA found an outlet for its frustration in acts of brutality and terror by individual formations within their own localities. It was particularly to the SA that Hitler directed his appeals for recognition that the revolution had ended. The "Supreme Leader of the SA" by no means had the SA in hand.

Meanwhile the problem had passed beyond the stage where appeals could solve it. The fact remained that the swelling SA was without a task, and that it watched the development of the new régime with growing displeasure. From the first the SA had been an independent organisation parallel to, but independent of, the Party. The "Law for protecting the unity of Party and State" of December 1st 1933, which had promoted the "Fuehrer's representative" and the "Chief of Staff of the SA" (i.e. the chiefs of the Party political organisation and the SA military organisation respectively) to be Reich Ministers, confirmed this independence quite clearly.

Roehm shared his men's dissatisfaction with the course of the revolution. He was not prepared to accept the passive role allotted him. He knew the power which the SA placed in his hands and did everything to enlarge it by increasing the number of armed formations. In all this he was far from wanting to be disloyal to Hitler. But he found Hitler more and more involved in a contradiction of their common aims, and from this concluded that he must prepare the SA to carry out one day by force what Hitler had neglected to achieve. This was what the call for the "second revolution" meant.

Roehm's criticism of the course of the revolution was centred on the question of the future German Army. He despised the Reichswehr leadership, which he considered reactionary, and he knew that Hitler shared his views. That Hitler collaborated with it instead of removing it appeared to him a grave mistake. Roehm wanted to prepare the way for a fusion of the Reichswehr and the SA into a militia, a National Socialist People's Army, which would be the crowning achievement of the Nazi victory.

Besides this, Roehm must have had further reservations. He had a social conscience and took the socialism of the Nazi programme seriously; it can hardly have pleased him to see this aspect of National Socialism completely overshadowed after the resignation of Gregor Strasser. It is also said that he opposed the dissolution of the trade unions, which Ley undertook on Hitler's orders by forcibly occupying the trade union headquarters on May 2nd 1933. It also seems that Roehm differed from Hitler on foreign policy, and that he advocated a quick understanding with the Western Powers, particularly France. Finally, it seems obvious that when his relationship with Hitler became critical, a man who liked to see the world arranged in a neat military hierarchic order, and who had always remained a convinced monarchist, must have had grave doubts as to the dangers of unlimited arbitrary power contained in Hitler's dictatorship. The "primacy of the soldier" over the politician, which Roehm had advocated long before the Party came to power, demanded a different solution of things.

Roehm was a revolutionary of the old school. He can hardly have envisaged the Nazi revolution as differing from the revolutions of the history books: a process beginning with the *avant-garde* storming the barricades—a phase of unavoidable bloodshed to be quickly overcome—the overthrow of the old order and its replacement by a new one. He never saw the SA as anything but the "storm-troopers" of such a revolution in the old style.

If Hitler ever shared these ideas, he had long moved away from them. More cunning, more subtle, more modern than the old-fashioned, straightforward, "pig-headed" Roehm, he saw very different possibilities in the political situation with which he came to grips after assuming the chancellorship. Almost automatically the methods of "cold" revolution had presented themselves: sham legality, lurking terror, the channelling of the revolution into measured, isolated actions whose significance could only be seen in mutual relationship, the outsmarting and deception not only of the enemy but also of the friend. Instinct may also have told him that modern revolutions no longer storm barricades, but can be conducted by a slow process of attrition, more profound in its effect than the method of any revolution hitherto, since it affects not only institutions but the human substance as well.

But what Roehm might at first have regarded as a mere quarrel over method was of fundamental importance to

47

Hitler. He did not oppose the demand for a "second revolution" because he rejected its predictable horrors, but because he mistrusted its purpose. Roehm recognised this too late. A passionate conspirator, he would hardly have campaigned so openly and uninhibitedly for the "second revolution" if he had not been convinced earlier on that Hitler shared his aims.

What settled matters for Hitler was Roehm's main demand that the Reichswehr be handed over to the SA, which would then be made the army of the new State. With the inner distribution of power as it then was, Hitler shrank back from the idea. At the same time Roehm's demand touched the old problem of the Nazi movement—the rivalry between the SA and the Party. To put the SA in the place of the Reichswehr would have meant giving it the most powerful position in the State. Hitler could only have done it against the staunch resistance of the leading Party functionaries. Finally, he saw in Roehm's demand a threat to his own position. The thought of Roehm beside him as commander of the entire armed forces was disturbing. Roehm was the only one of his immediate entourage whom he never had been able to captivate by his strange fascination. After Gregor Strasser went, Roehm was indeed his only rival.

Hitler was a temporiser who often put off awkward decisions for weeks and even months. He hesitated in the case of Roehm, too. But after the spring of 1934 forces were at work in whose interest it lay to exacerbate the conflict. Fully appreciating Hitler's mentality they engineered a situation in which he was forced to make up his mind. There is no doubt that Roehm, on his side, toyed with the idea of carrying out his "second revolution" even against Hitler himself, after Hitler, as he saw it, had betrayed the idea. But it is equally certain that he and his fellow conspirators were far from ready for action on June 30th.

Roehm's enemies were the Party on the one hand and the Reichswehr on the other. The Party's dislike for Roehm was traditional, and it became all the greater when the Party and not the SA achieved ascendancy after the seizure of power. When it became apparent that Roehm was not going to resign himself to the situation, it became a very personal matter, for the leading Party functionaries felt a threat to their individual share in the newly won power. Roehm's most influential enemies within the Party were probably Goering, Goebbels and Hess. In Goering's shadow, his then subordinates, Himmler and Heydrich, were also working for the downfall of the SA Chief of Staff. They already had their own ideas about the SS as the Nazi *corps d'élite*.

The Reichswehr's grounds for enmity were obvious. The amateur competition of the SA was tiresome; the person of its Chief of Staff suspect. Roehm and the SA were responsible for the lingering terror of the revolution. The Reichswehr was fully informed about his plans and had no illusion about the danger they presented. It thought it might draw the fangs of the revolution by helping to bring about Roehm's fall and putting the SA in its proper place. It was therefore necessary to drive a wedge between Roehm and Hitler, and to convince the latter that he needed the Reichswehr and could rely on it. The Reichswehr was well placed in this respect, since its two representatives—the War Minister, von Blomberg, and the Chief of the Wehrmacht Office, von Reichenau—were not subject to Hitler's distrust of officers in general. Blomberg had been an unexpected stroke of luck for Hitler. An outsider among his fellow officers, he had soon fallen under the Fuehrer's spell and become his uncritical admirer. Reichenau was even more important. As a convinced Nazi he was the only influential officer of the Reichswehr to have been in touch with Hitler before 1933. He was very ambitious, brutal and politically gifted—the intellectual superior of his Minister, and an officer of more modern stamp. Just as Schleicher had for a long time influenced the policy of the Republic, so it was Reichenau and not his Minister who, working from a back room, directed Reichswehr policy.

Hitler wanted a strong army. Rearmament was a cardinal theme of his foreign policy, which from the moment he came to power aimed at freedom of manœuvre. It was also a domestic problem in so far as it involved the political attitude of the future Wehrmacht. Would the Reichswehr follow him politically? His experience since coming to power gave more grounds for encouragement than he can have expected. Its command had proved compliant and willing. He knew very well that rearmament was above all a technical problem requiring for its solution the military expertise, technical knowledge and specialisation of the officer corps. Was he to risk this capital by a "co-ordination" of the Reichswehr with Roehm's SA, with its attendant violence and bloodshed?

Into all this must have entered yet another question, which directly affected Hitler's personal status: the question of Hindenburg's successor. Since the spring of 1934 the initiates had known that the Reich President was unlikely to survive the year. And as any settlement about his successor involved the supreme command of the Reichswehr, there could be no solution unacceptable to it. Did Hitler buy the Reichswehr's consent to amalgamating the offices of Chancellor and President in himself by sacrificing Roehm and the SA? The question cannot be answered to this day.

In the second half of June some events which are not quite clear seem to have led to a situation where the Reichswehr and parts of the SA came face to face in a state of immediate alert, each prepared for the other to open hostilities. Roehm had not planned a *putsch* for June 30th. But the SA was on the alert because it thought the military measures ordered for the Reichswehr on the pretext of an imminent SA *putsch* were preparations for an attack on itself. This state of affairs must have been brought about deliberately. The atmosphere was so tense at the time that a word or two of false information through the appropriate channels was enough to make action by either side imminent in any case. The situation was just what was wanted to make Hitler translate his decision into deeds.

There can be no doubt as to the identity of the stage managers. Reichenau was one, certainly. His position enabled him to play this game in the name of the Reichswehr, though he can hardly have done it without the knowledge of his immediate superior, Blomberg. The principal executioners, Goering and Himmler, must also have been party. They alone had the necessary apparatus to set the scene, i.e. the secret police, whose chief was Goering but which was actually commanded by Himmler under Goering's orders. Finally, their most important helper was Heydrich, whose position as chief of the Berlin office of the secret police put him immediately at the centre of events. Their co-operation bore fruit when

Hitler unleashed the action against the SA leaders in the early hours of June 30th.

There was never any attempt at legal procedure. Anyone suspected of complicity was shot without trial. Hitler himself took action in Munich, while Goering carried out his orders in Berlin. In both places the police and the SS were the executioners. Although the official German News Agency reported on July 2nd that the action had lasted only twenty-four hours, and Hitler declared next day that it had been completed during the night of July 1st, the murders continued for almost three days. The law of July 3rd by which the Reich Government subsequently legalised the murders, declaring them to be acts in "self-defence of the State", referred to "measures carried out on June 30th, July 1st and July 2nd".

In a self-contradictory speech of justification on July 13th, Hitler gave the number of victims as seventy-seven. In fact there were at least double, and perhaps three times, that number. It will never be possible to establish the exact total. Among them were not only the SA leaders devoted to Roehm but also numerous enemies of the régime. In his speech, Hitler mentioned only Gregor Strasser and Generals von Schleicher and von Bredow. It may be taken for certain that Hitler never forgave Strasser for his initiative in 1932 in holding talks with Schleicher, which nearly caused a split in the Party. At the same time Schleicher must have incurred the implacable hatred of Hitler and the Party. There is no proof that Schleicher had any contacts with Roehm or that his one-time collaborator Bredow acted as a go-between with foreign Powers. The official account that Schleicher was shot for offering armed resistance to arrest was a blatant lie. Schleicher and his wife were murdered in cold blood. Among victims whose names were at first only rumoured were the former Bavarian State Commissioner von Kahr, the Berlin Catholic leader Erich Klausener, and two of Papen's close collaborators —his Press officer, von Bose, and the conservative journalist Edgar Jung.

The official version of the event spoke of "crushing the Roehm revolt" and accused the murdered men of high treason. The allegation that they had maintained subversive relations with representatives of a foreign Power—generally understood to mean the French Ambassador in Berlin, François-Poncet—was later withdrawn because of protests by the French Government. The report dwelt at length on the moral depravity of Roehm and his circle—as if the facts had not been known for years and Hitler had not condoned them. The general public felt relief at the end of the lingering SA terror and the threat of a "second revolution". Many were frightened by the brutality of the action; but many more were prepared to overlook it or explain it as a victory for the good powers of Nazism over the evil. Nobody could see through the whole complexity of what had happened; and few indeed foresaw the consequences.

The Consequences of June 30th

THE thirtieth of June meant the end of the Nazi "revolution" in the crude sense in which its supporters had understood it. The murder of the adherents of the "second revolution" silenced all restless elements. At one stroke the various forces which had been on the move since the accession to power were fixed in those positions in which we shall find them for years to come. Their attitude to the events of June 30th determined their places for the future.

Hitler himself emerged from the action with greatly increased power and prestige. Having rid himself of his only rival, he was without a single rebel among the leading Nazis from now until the end of the régime. After Hindenburg's death on August 2nd 1934 the powers of the President were smoothly transferred to him. He thereby became both Head of State and Supreme Commander of the Reichswehr, holding in his hand a plenitude of power that was unique. In one of those plebiscites which the Nazi régime handled with so much virtuosity, the arrangement gained the consent of 38·4 million out of 45·5 million voters.

The Reichswehr seemed to be the true victor of June 30th. Hitler did everything to keep up this appearance. In his speech of justification on July 13th he stated emphatically that the Reichswehr was the only armed force in the State and that he intended to preserve it as a "non-political instrument". But the Reichswehr had little cause for satisfaction at Hitler's demonstrations of favour. The thirtieth of June had thrown discredit on the integrity of its leadership. It is true that the Reichswehr took no active part in the measures of June 30th and the two days following. But those who in the Reichswehr's name took part in the preparations must have known they were risking the murders which followed. They cannot be exonerated of joint responsibility. The quiet acceptance by the Reichswehr of the murder of two of its generals, in spite of outraged protests from the officer corps, shows that in some sinister way it felt itself implicated. Inevitably this produced a rift in the officer corps, which believed its chief bond lay in a common morality. Hitler's quiet counter-revolution managed to sow the seeds of disintegration in the last surviving social unit in Germany. It was his greatest triumph of June 30th. With the new oath of August 2nd, which no longer bound the Reichswehr to "Nation and Fatherland" but to the Fuehrer in person, Adolf Hitler was able to bind the Army completely to his régime and render resistance of any kind extremely difficult.

But the Party could assess the outcome of the action against Roehm with justified satisfaction. The old quarrel with the SA over precedence within the movement had finally been decided in its favour. At the highest level it was now only Hess, the chief of the political organisation, who represented the Party in the cabinet, since Hitler had repealed the law which conferred on the SA Chief of Staff the status of a Reich Minister. The SA received a new Chief of Staff, Lutze, an officer seconded from the Reichswehr. It soon became a mass organisation without influence or political importance, and its past seemed obliterated.

Hitler's gratitude to the SS took a momentous form. "In view of the great services of the SS, particularly in connection with the thirtieth of June", he lifted it from its previous position of subordination to the SA and promoted it to be an independent organisation within the framework of the Party, subject to his own immediate authority. With this gesture began the great rise of Himmler and the SS, one of the most important developments of the coming years.

The elevation of the SS to be the mighty organisation which characterised the future of the Nazi régime is symbolical of the change of character the whole régime underwent with the thirtieth of June. Having publicly established cold-blooded murder as a legitimate means of policy, it could no longer escape the consequences of its crime. From now on there is an atmosphere of blown fuses about Nazi policy. Power and violence have become inextricably linked. The Nazi *weltanschauung* of Hitler and his associates reveals itself as a pretence and a device. More and more the unequivocal aim is not the realisation of an idea but *power*.

1933–8
ON THE ROAD TO THE "GREATER GERMAN REICH"

The Beginnings of a Nazi Foreign Policy

W HEN Hitler came to power, the international situation was not unfavourable to Germany. Step by step the foreign policy of the Republic had succeeded in lightening the severe conditions which the victors of the first world war had imposed on Germany in the Treaty of Versailles. Germany's isolation in Europe had been ended. She had amassed a considerable capital of confidence. Reparations had ceased. In the disarmament discussions of 1932, Germany, after pointing out that she was the only country to have carried out the disarmament obligations of the Treaty of Versailles, had demanded equality. On December 11th 1932, a few weeks before Hitler became Chancellor, Germany's claim to equality of rights had been recognised, at least in principle, in a joint declaration by England, France and Italy.

Of all the European Powers, only Poland had remained hostile and had repeatedly caused the statesmen of the Republic anxiety. Relations continued to be uneasy with France, which consistently opposed German revisionism; but they were much better with Britain and Italy. Germany could also count on goodwill in the United States. Amicable relations with the Soviet Union had become almost traditional with the Weimar Republic after the Treaty of Rapallo in 1922. They were not disturbed by Germany's internal struggle against

Communism, and they were particularly important for Germany from an economic standpoint.

Nevertheless, after the sharp tumble which Germany had taken after the first world war, there was still much to be desired: enough, that is, to prevent the Republic from bringing its undoubted successes to the notice of an impatient public and taking the wind out of the sails of Nazi propaganda, which regarded the "struggle against Versailles" as one of its most effective planks. The full extent of the political mobility regained by Germany since 1919 was not generally appreciated until Hitler, in his early days of power, began to make capital out of it. Time and again the public gave him personal credit for what was really the result of protracted labour by his predecessors.

Hitler, who had never been abroad and spoke no foreign language, regarded foreign policy as his personal preserve. While prepared to concede his collaborators considerable scope in home affairs, he had no liking for their advice on external matters. As time went on, his dislike of career diplomatists led him to eliminate, as far as he could, the influence of the German Foreign Service. In his early work of propaganda *Mein Kampf* he had already set out his conception of German foreign policy. He admired the historical achievements of England, in which he saw proof of his theory of the superiority of the Germanic race. He admired Fascist Italy and its creator, Mussolini. He saw an alliance with England and Italy as Germany's security for the future against the "unrelenting, mortal enemy" France, as well as against Soviet Russia, at whose expense, in particular, he wished to enlarge Germany's "living space". Austria, the country of his birth, was for him an integral part of Germany, and her reunification with the Reich "a life's task, to be carried out by every means". In the first years of Nazi foreign policy it looked as if Hitler had abandoned most of the fundamentals of his programme. Only later did it become apparent that it was precisely in foreign politics that he had held fast to his early beliefs.

To begin with, Hitler continued the foreign policy of his predecessors. He made no experiments, particularly as Germany's international prestige was much affected by events at home. The question of disarmament remained the foremost topic of international debate, soon to be dominated by the fact that Hitler was secretly rearming. The second Geneva Disarmament Conference faced the difficult task of effectively granting Germany the equality of rights open to all nations under a system of security. MacDonald's disarmament plan, submitted on March 16th 1933, met with only qualified support from Germany and was rejected by France. On October 9th, after interim Anglo-French discussions, a new proposal was submitted to the Conference, by which Germany would not be granted a status of equality until after a transitional period of four years. On October 14th 1933 Hitler replied to this proposal by announcing Germany's withdrawal from both the Disarmament Conference and the League of Nations. In a plebiscite on November 12th 88 per cent of the electorate gave their approval to this step, little foreseeing the consequences. One of the first of these was Hitler's order to accelerate rearmament.

Germany's withdrawal from the League reversed the whole trend by which she had emerged in the twenties from the isolated position of loser in the war to re-enter the circle of

European nations. By rejecting the system of collective security which under French leadership had governed European politics since Versailles, Hitler was risking a new isolation. He never ceased to protest his love of peace and to make proposals for disarmament. But at the same time he made it clear that he preferred the principle of bilateral agreements to that of securing peace by multilateral treaties.

The first example of such a bilateral agreement was the German-Polish non-aggression pact of January 26th 1934. From this pact Nazi foreign policy gained a twofold advantage. It put an end to latent tensions on the German eastern frontier (which proved to be of advantage to Hitler four years later, when he could act against Austria and Czechoslovakia without fear of Polish intervention). At the same time, it tore a sizeable hole in the French system of alliances. Admittedly the treaty obligations between France and Poland remained in force. But for France the fact that Poland had reached a diplomatic understanding with Germany meant a great reduction in the value of her traditional alliance. Poland's motive was mainly uneasiness about the Soviet Union. Her fear of becoming the Soviet deployment area in case of a Franco-German conflict was not unfounded, since events within Germany had led to signs of a Franco-Russian *rapprochement.*

On April 17th 1934 the French Foreign Minister, Barthou, declared in a note to Britain that in view of Germany's re-armament contrary to her obligations under the peace treaty, France felt that further discussions about disarmament and German equality were useless. Under Barthou the subsequent aim of French foreign policy was to create safeguards against the growing power of Germany by including Russia in the

French system of alliances. The Soviet Union, on the other hand, had reason to seek an *approchement* with the Western Powers since her friendly relations with Germany, sustained over a decade, had somewhat cooled as a result of Nazi foreign policy. In May 1934 France and the Soviet Union opened talks about a system of East European pacts, which was visualised as an eastern extension of the Locarno Pact of 1925, and which was to include Germany also. In September 1934 the Soviet Union joined the League of Nations as a result of the Western reorientation of her policy. Almost simultaneously the German Government declared that it would take no part in the projected Eastern Pact, and that it continued to regard bilateral agreements as the best method of securing peace.

After the assassination of Barthou and King Alexander of Yugoslavia in Marseilles in October 1934, Barthou's successor, Laval, more or less continued his policy, which had aimed at winning Italy to the ranks of the anti-revisionists by means of a Yugoslav-Italian settlement. In January 1935 he gained Mussolini's assent to the proposed pact. In a joint Anglo-French declaration of February 3rd, Germany was once more invited to take part in the proposed pact system and so make possible an international solution of the rearmament problem. Hitler replied non-committally at first, not without once again advocating bilateral agreements. A few weeks later he decided on a measure which the world took for his final answer, and by which all efforts for an Eastern Pact embracing Germany were rendered useless: on March 16th he announced general conscription, thereby officially admitting what the world already knew, although it had been done in secret—that Germany was rearming He justified this step by saying that he had to protect Germany from the threats implicit in British and French rearmament measures. France had recently re-introduced two years' service for a number of annual classes, and the British Government had published a White Paper pointing to German rearmament as justification for an increase in defence expenditure.

Britain, France and Italy protested. On April 11th the heads of their three governments met at Stresa, to condemn the German action and reaffirm their faith in the system of collective security based on the League of Nations. The League adopted the attitude of the Stresa Conference and contemplated sanctions against Germany. On May 2nd, France concluded a mutual assistance pact with the Soviet Union, while the latter entered into an alliance with Czechoslovakia on May 16th. Both pacts were plainly directed against Germany. Hitler seemed isolated by the embrace of a European coalition.

But the sanctions were never put into effect, and the unity of Stresa went no farther than oratory. Hitler was proved right in the face of those who had warned him that the introduction of conscription would provoke determined, and possibly warlike, counter-measures by the Great Powers. On the contrary, in no time at all he was able to claim a remarkable success for his policy of bilateral alliances which only seemed to prove the discord of the Western Powers and encouraged him to continue in the same way. On June 18th 1935 Britain signed a naval agreement with Germany, which laid down the strengths of the British and German fleets in the ratio of 100 to 35, with parity in submarines. Thus she tacitly accepted German rearmament, which shortly before she had condemned at Stresa. Among British statesmen the pressure of world events, particularly in the Far East, began to encourage the idea that peace in Europe could best be preserved by appeasing Hitler with concessions.

Soon the transitory nature of the unity of Stresa became clearer still. In the autumn of 1935 Italy made war on Abyssinia. Mussolini conducted and completed his campaign in spite of League of Nations sanctions, and by the summer of 1936 Abyssinia had been annexed. It was during this period that the relationship between Italy and Germany was cemented. For years Mussolini had evaded Hitler's advances and kept his distance. This was not only due to his personal reservations about Hitler. Much more important was the Austrian question between the two countries. It took the Abyssinian campaign to bring about a *rapprochement*. Germany helped Italy with raw materials, thereby reducing the effect of the league's sanctions. The occasion for still closer collaboration was provided by the Spanish Civil War, which began on July 18th 1936. Italy and Germany intervened on the side of Franco's insurgents, thus ensuring their ultimate victory over the Republicans, who were supported by the Soviet Union.

During the Abyssinian campaign, and under cover of the political confusion it had caused, Hitler had risked a highly dangerous move: on March 7th 1936 German troops marched into the Rhineland, designated a demilitarised zone by the Treaty of Versailles. Hitler justified this new breach of the treaty by arguing that he had to protect Germany from the effect of the Franco-Soviet Pact, which had been ratified by the French Chamber on February 27th, and which was incompatible with the Locarno Treaty. Once again he was

E

proved right against all warnings, particularly from his generals. The only outcome was paper protests.

The first phase of Nazi foreign policy ended with a further spectacular success. On November 25th 1936 Hitler signed a treaty with Japan—the so-called "Anti-Comintern Pact"— for their common struggle against the Third International. Its propaganda effect was greater than its political substance. But it paved the way for future German-Japanese collaboration with far-reaching possibilities.

In less than four years Hitler had achieved full freedom of movement for Germany and had practically invalidated the Treaty of Versailles. He had shattered the system of European collective pacts initiated by France, and he had gained the partnership of Poland, Italy and Japan with his policy of bilateral agreements. He might have been taken for a politician of genius. But only if one accepted the basic assumptions of his political actions: the conviction that one's own nation was the most important in the world, regardless of the claims of any other, and the assumption that breach of contract and the use of force were legitimate means of policy.

The Years of Preparation (1934-8)

INSIDE Germany, the dramatic events of the summer of 1934 were followed by years in which the régime consolidated itself, dyed public life with the colour of Nazism, and tried to imbue the German people with its spirit. Whatever there had been of a "movement" now became rigid as a result of its growing dependence, at first unnoticeable, on central direction. Every aspect of living was brought under mammoth organisations and "co-ordinated" with the intentions of the leadership. A monotonous uniformity weighed down on it. A succession of laws prescribed for young Germans their progress from the "Hitler Youth" via "National Labour Service" to service with the armed forces. Under the leadership of the radical-materialist Ley, the "German Labour Front" and its recreational organisation "Strength through Joy" had taken the place of the trade unions. Bodies like the National Socialist League for Public Welfare and the National Socialist Women's League covered the entire country with their finely woven net of functionaries and, whatever their sometimes innocent-sounding objects, effectively served the Party in the control of each individual. Even intellectual and cultural life was forced into the Party mould by means of Goebbels's Reich Chamber of Culture.

Within the State machinery, Himmler and Heydrich pressed on with the development of the SS into an all-powerful "political bodyguard of the National Socialist State". An important stage in this development was reached on June 17th 1936 by Hitler's order for the amalgamation of all police forces in a single State Police under Himmler. At the same time the SS began to build up big military formations on the model of the "Leibstandarte Adolf Hitler", which had originally been designed for the Fuehrer's personal protection. Such were the measures which gave the lie to Hitler's assurance that the Army was to be the only armed force in the State, and they created fresh tension between Army and Party. The SS began to develop its own apparatus within that of the Nazi Government. It worked on more modern and efficient lines than any of the other organisations, and its ambition was to become the nucleus of Nazi power.

The systematic persecution of opponents had never ceased, although the political opposition had been so emphatically silenced during the revolution that it no longer constituted a danger. Persecution became a function of the power apparatus, and when actual enemies of political importance were no longer available it was turned on potential or imaginary ones. The concentration camps, which had apparently been intended for the temporary detention of political enemies during the first weeks of power, became essential institutions and were constantly enlarged. Within their closely guarded privacy the SS inflicted on the prisoners the cold-blooded system of terror which was to become the symbol of Nazi power.

Amongst its victims, the German Jews suffered most. Hitler did not invent anti-Semitism. It flared up, as it had done from time to time in many centuries, including the nineteenth, and not only in Germany; it was an old emotion which found pseudo-rational support in modern materialist theories, without, however, being able to create a "movement". It seems clear that it was neither the convincing force of these racial theories nor a chance influence by some of their disciples on the young and immature Hitler which really determined his way of thought and action. It was rather the tendency of a socially uprooted individual to resentment which caused him an enormous anti-Semitic hate-complex, which then, in turn, searched for an ideological justification. This tendency may have been encouraged by personal experience, and certainly it was fully developed by the general situation. For the events of 1918 created the unique need of a scapegoat on whom to shift the guilt of defeat; a defeat which a proud nation, deeply wounded in its self-esteem, refused to accept as a fact of history. A large part of this dejected nation was more or less prepared to see "November criminals and Jews" as the authors of its "undeserved" misery. Hitler himself became obsessed by this "discovery". At the same time he divined the tactical advantages of a potential anti-Semitic bias in a movement setting out to appeal to sections of the population which had been forced down the social scale by inflation and economic crisis. Later the Jews were again and again to provide the "enemy" which seems so absolutely indispensable to the totalitarian State. Venomous anti-Semitic propaganda and agitation was followed, somewhat hesitantly in the early years, by direct action. The crowning anti-Semitic measure of the years 1933-4 was the enactment of the so-called "Nuremberg Laws" of September 1935. They formed the nucleus of a long succession of Nazi decrees systematically depriving German

Jewry of all civil rights and so placing it at anybody's mercy. With these venomous laws the régime embarked on the course which was to lead, after the international political victories of 1938, to the pogroms of the nights of November 9th and 10th of the same year, and was to end, consistently enough, in the extermination measures carried out during the war.

Nazism was bound by its very nature to be the enemy of Christianity, refusing, as it did, to recognise the pre-eminence of the individual's conscience beyond the orders of the Fuehrer and duties to the Party. Soon the Churches, too, became the target of systematic persecution. The Nazis' friendly attitude towards Christianity in the first weeks of the "national awakening" was based on misunderstanding, or else was a deliberate deception. On July 20th 1933 the Nazi Government had entered into a concordat with the Vatican. But ignoring its stipulations, it unleashed a shameless anti-Catholic propaganda campaign, which gave free rein to the resentment of the numerous renegade Catholics among the Party leaders. As for the Protestants, hopes were at first entertained that they could be made to toe the line and be re-formed as an obedient State Church. But attempts to force this through with the aid of the Nazi "German Christians" proved fruitless and gave rise to counter-forces which, as the "Confessional Church", courageously attacked the subversion of the Christian faith. Both Protestants and Catholics took their share in awakening the faithful to the irreconcilable antithesis between Christianity and National Socialism, and so made them ready for spiritual resistance.

If the German people remained loyal to the State in spite

of growing oppression by the practitioners of totalitarian power and the increasing alienation of life by the Nazi system, it was due above all to the success of the régime in its economic and foreign policy. Rearmament, government contracts and the clever finance and external trade policy of Schacht had led—with the help of the passing of the world depression—to a surprisingly quick recovery of the German economy. Above all, mass unemployment, the most pressing problem of Weimar days, had been solved within a few years. These were achievements of benefit to everybody. On the other hand, the obliging attitude of other countries who sent their statesmen to Hitler and, seemingly undeterred by his breaches of faith, continued to make new treaties with him, was taken as a sign that the Nazi State and its achievements were recognised abroad and even admired. Many a doubt in Germany as to the honesty of Nazi ends and means was silenced by the feeble attitude (or so it seemed) of the outside world.

But what *were* the ends of Nazism? Hitler never stopped assuring the world that he wanted peace. But all the measures he took to restore the economy, to raise production, increase exports, secure raw materials, build up new industries and establish the self-sufficiency of agriculture were designed for war. Did Hitler fear an attack on Germany? On September 9th 1936 at Nuremberg, announcing the second Four-Year Plan, which summarised economic preparations for war, he spoke of the possibility of a "Bolshevik invasion"; but this was in the tradition of Nazi propaganda and, at this time, purely demagogic. Or did Hitler himself want a war? We know now that by the autumn of 1937, if not earlier, he was prepared to "risk using force", i.e. to make war, at relatively short notice.

For on November 5th 1937, in the presence of the Foreign Minister, von Neurath, Hitler explained his plans for external policy to his closest military collaborators, Blomberg, Fritsch, Raeder and Goering, in an address lasting several hours, of which his Wehrmacht aide-de-camp Hossbach made a memorandum a few days later. He underlined the importance of his statement by adding that he "wished it to be regarded as his testament in case of death". He defined the aim of German policy as to "safeguard and preserve the nation and its growth". This, he said, could only be achieved by a solution of the problem of "overcrowding", i.e. by achieving greater "living space" for the German people, not in colonial territories overseas, but "in the immediate proximity of the Reich in Europe". There was only one way of achieving this, "the way of force". It was his "irrevocable decision" to solve Germany's "living space problem"—at the latest by 1943-5, but earlier still if the political circumstances were favourable, and perhaps even in 1938. In any event, strategic considerations made the overthrow and annexation of Czechoslovakia and Austria the inevitable first steps.

Some of his remarks may have been intended to spur his hesitant generals to speed up military preparations; nevertheess, the further course of events showed Hitler to have been expressing the ideas which guided his future policy. An entirely new note had been struck. He foresaw the development of German rearmament to the point where he could include military force in his plans for foreign policy. From now on he seems to have waited impatiently for the chance to play the card of Germany's military might accumulated over the past five years.

There is no doubt that Hitler was extremely displeased when Blomberg and Fritsch replied to his address with political and military objections expressing a sharp and fundamental difference of views. Their reaction was but one of a series of disappointments which he had suffered in his relations with the command of the armed forces. These relations had certainly not developed in accordance with the close understanding behind his decisions in the summer of 1934. Since assuming supreme command after the death of Hindenburg, he had met with resistance by the generals on several occasions. He felt they had been too hesitant in carrying out rearmament. They had entertained political doubts about the moment for introducing conscription, and technical doubts as to how it was to be carried out. They had advised against the occupation of the Rhineland as being still too great a risk. The doubts of Blomberg and Fritsch about his plans for conquest were but one more instance of that caution and hesitancy which irritated him because it hindered him in his plans, and which he despised because he had already so often triumphed over it.

In the light of his experiences Hitler decided on sweeping changes in the personnel of the Wehrmacht leadership, and they took place in highly questionable circumstances at the beginning of 1938. The occasion was a scandal involving the War Minister, von Blomberg. In January 1938 Blomberg had married for a second time. Hitler and Goering had been witnesses at his wedding. Shortly afterwards it became known that Blomberg's bride was a lady of doubtful reputation. On January 24th Goering presented the evidence to Hitler, who decided that Blomberg must relinquish his office. Hitler seems to have been surprised at this turn of affairs, which scarcely left him with any alternative.

But the matter did not rest there. By January 25th a Gestapo file was lying on Hitler's desk, incriminating von Fritsch, the Commander in Chief of the Army, in homosexual activities. Hitler had seen the same file before, in 1936. At that time he had refused to take up the matter, and ordered the file to be destroyed. We now know that at this juncture Hitler himself had the file reconstructed in order to bring about the fall of Fritsch, who was already highly inconvenient in his present position and would be even more so as Blomberg's successor. Hitler relieved Fritsch of his command and forced him to resign from the Army even before a court of inquiry could investigate the matter. As it turned out, the court of inquiry established Fritsch's innocence. His defence was able to prove that the incriminating evidence did not concern him, but an ex-officer of the name of von Frisch. In the end the Gestapo witness, a man with several previous convictions, admitted that he had lied under pressure of Gestapo threats. But the verdict did nothing to revoke Fritsch's dismissal. He had the greatest difficulty in being rehabilitated—and then not publicly—by Hitler. On the outbreak of war he accompanied his regiment without power of command, seeking his death, which he met before Warsaw.

The driving personalities behind this odious game were Goering, Himmler and Heydrich. Goering pursued personal aims: he wanted Blomberg's job, or at least the joint supreme command of the Army and Air Force. Himmler and Heydrich, in the interests of the SS, welcomed anything which would compromise its military rival and weaken the position of the military leadership. The trio was furthermore backed by the Party's old resentment of the Army. The Party welcomed the downfall of Blomberg and Fritsch as a kind of revenge for the Wehrmacht's triumph of June 30th 1934. The Wehrmacht accepted it without a murmur. But Goering's hopes were not fulfilled and he had to be content with his appointment as a Field-Marshal.

Hitler had used the situation which chance and calculation had placed into his hands to make decisive inroads upon the Wehrmacht's independence. He performed a final act of "co-ordination", hoping thereby to do away with some of the resistance which had become so troublesome. He abolished the office of War Minister, in which Blomberg had hitherto deputised for Hitler as supreme commander of the armed forces, and assumed this function himself. From the "Wehrmacht Office" in the War Ministry he formed the Oberkommando der Wehrmacht or OKW (Supreme Command of the Armed Forces) to be his personal staff as supreme commander. At the same time the new Supreme Command took over the War Ministry's work. He appointed as its chief a compliant general, Keitel, who had succeeded Reichenau as Chief of the Wehrmacht Office in 1935. General von Brauchitsch became Fritsch's successor as Commander-in-Chief of the Army in circumstances which made him dependent upon Hitler.

This new arrangement was strangely incongruous in so far as the newly created OKW was not made senior to the commanders of the three services but equal with them. This led to countless rivalries and was to have disastrous consequences in the war. But it was entirely in accordance with Hitler's principle of creating within the same department competing authorities, so as to counteract the influence of individuals and lend greater weight to his personal decisions.

Hitler combined the changes in the command of the armed forces with a whole series of personnel changes in the military and diplomatic field. The most important of these concerned the Foreign Ministry. Joachim von Ribbentrop, his diplomatic adviser of long standing and former Ambassador in London, became Foreign Minister—a change which meant that at last the Wilhelmstrasse, too, was included in the "co-ordination". To cover this with a smoke-screen, Hitler invented a "Privy Cabinet Council", ostensibly to advise him on foreign affairs, and made the outgoing Foreign Minister, von Neurath, its President. The Council never once met.

The German public was not informed of what had happened behind the scenes. On February 4th 1938 a communiqué merely announced the changes that had been made. How Hitler wanted them to be received becomes clear from two sentences entered in the diary of Jodl, Keitel's closest collaborator, on January 31st 1938: "Fuehrer wants to divert the searchlights from the Wehrmacht, keep Europe on tenterhooks, and by recasting various roles give the impression of a concentration of strength, not of a moment of weakness. Schuschnigg must not take courage but fright." During the impending visit of the Austrian Chancellor, Hitler meant to carry the question of German-Austrian unification a decisive step farther. A few weeks after the crisis over Blomberg and Fritsch he marched into Austria.

The Anschluss and its Origins

THE Anschluss had been of concern to both Germany and Austria since the end of the Great War and was supported in each country by adherents of the most divergent political creeds, including the Socialists. But the unification of the two German states was forbidden by the peace treaties, and the victorious Powers watched suspiciously to see that the relevant provisions were obeyed. Even a timid attempt to form a customs union came to grief with the opposition of the Western Powers in 1931.

The political revolution of 1933 transformed this problem. The question of unification, hitherto an issue between the Austrian and German governments on one side and the victorious Powers on the other, became a dispute between Hitler and the Austrian Government. The Austrian opponents of Nazism, especially the Catholics and Socialists, became opponents of the Anschluss project, which would now mean an Anschluss with the Hitler régime.

When Hitler came to power, he had an Austrian opponent in the authoritarian Government of Dollfuss, which was supported by the forces of the Catholic Right. Tension became apparent when Hitler used his large Austrian following in an attempt to exert influence on Austria's internal affairs. The Dollfuss Government proscribed the Nazi Party, and Hitler virtually closed the frontier by levying a tax of a thousand marks on all outward journeys. Austria was encouraged in her firm attitude by the support she received from Italy. Mussolini made clear his determination to guarantee Austrian independence by committing Italy, Austria and Hungary to a joint policy in the Danube basin by the Rome Protocols of March 17th 1934. England and France, together with Italy, had already given a kind of guarantee exactly a month before.

This support proved valid when with unofficial German help the Austrian Nazis attempted to stage a *putsch* in Vienna on July 25th 1934. Dollfuss was murdered, but the *putsch* collapsed in ignominy. The unequivocal attitude of the three great Powers—Mussolini went so far as to march troops to the Italian-Austrian frontier—obliged Hitler to withhold official support and to deny all connection between the German Government and events in the Austrian capital.

There followed a period of pronounced German restraint. Hitler sent Papen as Ambassador to Vienna with orders to re-establish normal relations with the Austrian Government under the new Chancellor, Schuschnigg. The Austrian Government had already received German proposals for an alliance in the summer of 1935. But the agreement was only signed on July 11th 1936, after the re-establishment of Germany's international position. Each Government assured the other that their relations would again become normal and friendly. Germany recognised Austria's full sovereignty, and Austria acknowledged herself to be a German state. Both parties promised to abstain from interference in each other's internal affairs; a promise specifically extended to cover the question of Austrian Nazism.

But Hitler had little cause to take the agreement seriously. For the European political situation developed further in his favour. England showed an increasing tendency towards acquiescence and appeasement. More important still was the gain of Mussolini's friendship as a result of the Abyssinian adventure. This weakened the position of the Austrian Government considerably. It could be predicted that in future neither England nor Italy would involve themselves so firmly in the Austrian question as they had done in 1934. So the German-Austrian agreement served Hitler as cover for the very thing which Schuschnigg had hoped it would prevent: he began once more to exert his influence on Austria's internal affairs and to further as much as possible the growth of the still illegal Nazi movement in the country. In the autumn of 1937 the point had been reached where the Schuschnigg Government was seriously afraid that Hitler would use the next opportunity to violate the agreement openly.

On January 30th 1939 Hitler stated retrospectively that "in January 1938" he had finally decided "to win for the six and a half million Austrian Germans the right of self-determination". Austria, as we have seen, had been in his mind when he dismissed Blomberg and Fritsch. Schuschnigg was about to pay Hitler a visit, for which Papen had been working some time. The Austrian Chancellor had agreed to it somewhat hesitantly on the advice of Mussolini. The meeting took place on February 12th 1938 on the Obersalzberg. Hitler made no attempt even to make it appear a discussion between equals. He put demands amounting to an ultimatum and threatened point blank to use force if Schuschnigg refused them. Schuschnigg largely yielded, consenting to the "Berchtesgaden Agreement", which subjugated Austria to German policy. The agreement demanded the closest collaboration in the military and international field, and secured for the Austrian Nazis a considerable share in the Government.

Schuschnigg made a last, desperate effort to save Austria's independence. On March 9th in Innsbruck he went against the advice of Mussolini and called for a plebiscite. In this the Austrian people were to pronounce for a "free and German Austria, independent and socially harmonious, Christian and united; for peace and employment, and the equality of all who profess their faith in the people and the Fatherland". Schuschnigg hoped this formula would win a considerable majority, thus giving him, in future contests with Hitler, that basis of authority on which Hitler had cast doubts at the Obersalzberg meeting. But Schuschnigg's precipitate call spelled the doom of his Government. Hitler decided to force his resignation by ordering military measures. On March 11th the Austrian President, Miklas, received an ultimatum threatening an invasion of Austria by the German Army unless Schuschnigg resigned at once. Schuschnigg did so on the evening of March 11th, and declared in a radio broadcast that he had yielded to force. The Government was taken over by Seyss-Inquart, and the same night German troops began to occupy Austria. To justify the invasion the German Government published a telegram composed in Berlin, in which Seyss-Inquart allegedly asked for the sending of German troops. Seyss-Inquart protested in vain at the misuse of his name.

Impressed by the jubilation which greeted the marching in

of the German Army, Hitler at once went farther than he had originally intended. On March 13th he announced the complete Anschluss of Austria to the German Reich. Hitherto this had been a somewhat more remote target: something he had thought possible only after an intermediate stage in which the governments of both countries would be unified in his own person as Chancellor.

Hitler could await the reaction of the Great Powers to all this with equanimity, being assured of the approval of Mussolini, whom he had informed as late as the evening of March 11th. France and England merely protested. Poland, obedient to her treaty with Germany, stayed silent. Such being the circumstances, Czechoslovakia could be put off with a promise that events in Austria would have no effect on herself. Hitler had foreseen these developments exactly and had chosen the right moment. Austria provided a triumphant vindication of his policy and methods.

What impressed world opinion and made counter-moves by foreign governments all the more difficult was the fact that a majority of the two peoples received their unification with acclaim. None of Hitler's political actions had ever found a more joyful echo at home. Satisfaction at seeing the old dream of a German national State at last fulfilled without bloodshed counted far more at the moment than doubts about Hitler's methods or fears about his next step.

F

1938–9

THE PROLOGUE TO THE
SECOND WORLD WAR

The End of Czechoslovakia

THE easy success in Austria encouraged Hitler to turn immediately to the other part of the task which he had set himself in solving the "living space" problem: the subjugation of Czechoslovakia. From the end of March 1938 onwards it was apparent that it occupied the centre of his political plans. He was not yet quite certain about the timing and method. But he began to make political and military preparations so as to be ready at the next favourable moment.

Officially Germany practised restraint towards Czechoslovakia. Just as in Austria, Hitler could rely on his followers there to render the situation ripe for German intervention. The weakness of the Czechoslovak State lay in its lack of a homogeneous population. It consisted of three ethnical groups: Czechs, Slovaks and Sudeten Germans. The Czechs had brought the state into being at the end of the Great War. From the beginning they had regarded themselves as the chief nationality and had neglected to make the two minorities feel that the country was theirs also. In consequence it had never lost in the latter's eye the character of an imposed institution. This became dangerous after 1933 when Nazism began to extend its influence across the frontier and awaken forces among the Sudeten Germans which threatened the artificial state with disruption. In spite of this there were no serious conflicts between Czechoslovakia and Nazi Germany until 1938. Although the majority of the Sudeten German population supported the Sudeten German Party under Konrad Henlein, the latter had hitherto been careful to avoid anything which might raise doubts about the loyalty of the Sudeten Germans to the Czechoslovak State.

The Anschluss created a new situation and provided a great stimulus for the Sudeten Germans. At the end of March, Henlein arrived in Berlin on a secret visit to receive instructions from Hitler and Ribbentrop and begin the close co-operation which would steer developments in Czechoslovakia in accordance with Hitler's plans. The restraint of the Sudeten Party was dropped. By increasing its demands on the Czechoslovak Government the party effected a quick deterioration of the internal situation. So great was the general nervousness that on May 20th, on the strength of unsubstantiated rumours about German troop movements, the Government announced mobilisation and thus considerably increased the tension. Hitler felt challenged and found it intolerable that the rest of the world should welcome the attitude of the Czech Government as a sign of strength. He prepared his plans in detail. In a secret directive to the Wehrmacht on May 30th he declared: "It is my irrevocable decision to break up Czechoslovakia by a military action within the foreseeable future." The draft, written on May 20th, had read: "It is not my intention to break up Czechoslovakia by a military action in the foreseeable future without provocation, unless an unavoidable development of the political situation within Czechoslovakia obliges us . . ." A little later he committed himself more definitely as to the timing when he said, again in a secret directive, that he was determined to use "any favourable political opportunity" for the "solution of the Czech question" from October 1st onwards. At the same time he defined what he regarded as a "favourable political opportunity": he would act only if he was firmly convinced, as in the case of the occupation of the Rhineland and of the Anschluss, "that France will not march and that therefore England will not intervene".

Soon after the Anschluss, England made it clear that she would enter into no obligations on the Czech question, and that she expected the Prague Government to make concessions to the Sudeten Germans. France was committed to Czechoslovakia by a treaty of 1924. But as to her readiness to stand by this treaty, it was important, in view of British reserve, to know whether the Soviet Union would ultimately stand by its obligations under the Soviet-Czechoslovak treaty of 1935. The Soviet Union assured the French Foreign Minister, Bonnet, that this would be the case. But the assurance was of little value, for Soviet help could only be effective if Poland and Rumania gave Soviet troops the right to march through their territory. Neither country was prepared to do this. They feared their Soviet neighbour as much as they feared Nazi Germany. Furthermore relations between Poland and Czechoslovakia were anything but cordial, and Poland hoped for certain territorial gains as a result of the latter's downfall.

Under these circumstances, Hitler saw nothing to prevent him from carrying out his preparations. In the course of the summer, tension between the Czechs and the Sudeten Germans assumed serious forms and began to express itself in bloodshed. Behind the growing unrest and the exaggerated reports of it in the German Press, it was possible to detect the deliberate hand of the Nazi leadership. Clearly the object was now to create a situation in Czechoslovakia which would serve as an excuse for German intervention to protect the Sudeten Germans.

In this explosive situation Britain took the initiative in an attempt to reach a settlement between the Czech and German elements. At the beginning of August Lord Runciman went to Prague. His efforts proved fruitless and he finally reported to the British Government that in his opinion a separation of the Sudeten Germans from the Czechs was the only solution. The Runciman Mission confirmed Hitler in his opinion that England would not risk a rupture on account of the Czechoslovak question. On September 12th, at the Party congress in Nuremberg, he came out openly with a threat of German intervention. This led the British Government to a new and unorthodox step. Chamberlain, the British Prime Minister, made an offer to visit Hitler in person. After Runciman had failed to mediate between Sudeten Germans and Czechs, Chamberlain was attempting to bring about a direct settlement between Hitler and the Prague Government. On September 15th he met Hitler on the Obersalzberg. Hitler demanded autonomy for the Sudeten Germans. Chamberlain agreed to advise the Czech Government to cede the Sudeten German areas to Germany. As the French Government concurred with the British attitude, the Czechoslovak Government saw no choice but to yield.

On September 22nd and 23rd Chamberlain had a further meeting with Hitler at Godesberg, bringing him the decision of the Prague Government. But Hitler now placed Chamberlain in a situation which amounted to a serious personal affront: he used the Western Powers' compliance as a means of blackmail and declared that the stipulations agreed on at the Obersalzberg meeting were insufficient. He asked for the satisfaction of Hungarian and Polish territorial claims against Czechoslovakia and for the immediate surrender of the Sudeten German territories without consultation on technical details. Chamberlain was dismayed. He passed on the new German demands to Prague, but this time without the recommendation of the French and British Governments. Prague, in consequence, refused them. In a speech in the Berlin Sportpalast on September 26th, Hitler left no doubt that he intended to act. War seemed imminent.

The British Government made a last effort to save the peace. On September 28th it approached Mussolini with a request for his intervention. Hitler's demands and Prague's concessions did not appear so far divergent as to exclude the chance of Italian intervention succeeding. The move was surprisingly successful. Adopting the British suggestion, Mussolini got in touch with Hitler and secured the latter's agreement to a conference of the four Powers, which was to take place in Munich on the following day. Within a few hours—England had approached Rome in the morning, and at lunch-time the invitations were sent out from Berlin—a completely new situation had been created. It was not merely deference to Mussolini that caused Hitler to yield. Britain's warning about what would happen if Germany marched, together with the mood of the German people, seems to have caused him last-minute doubts as to whether Germany was really ready for a military enterprise. Today we know that the British initiative in Rome saved him from a *coup d'état* which the Wehrmacht was ready to stage the moment he gave the order to attack Czechoslovakia. The Chief of Staff of the Army, Halder, was deeply involved in this plan.

At the Munich conference (September 29th–30th) Hitler, Mussolini, Chamberlain and Daladier agreed that Germany should take over the Sudeten German areas by stages during the first days of October. Czechoslovakia was to be given a guarantee for her new frontiers. But Germany and Italy were not prepared to give their guarantees until after the Hungarian and Polish claims on Czechoslovakia had been satisfied. On September 30th Chamberlain and Hitler signed an additional "Anglo-German Joint Declaration", in which both parties expressed their intention, for the sake of safeguarding European peace, of dealing in future with questions of common concern by "the method of consultation".

The world was able to breathe again. Chamberlain and Daladier were enthusiastically welcomed home as peacemakers. The German people, who had acclaimed both statesmen in Munich, were relieved of a nightmare. They had followed Hitler's bellicose policy, pursued in their name, with great anxiety. But once again Hitler's methods had won a triumphant success. Once again, in the face of all warnings, he seemed to have been correct in his prediction that the Western Powers would avoid a war at all costs.

From the outcome of Munich the world gained a fleeting illusion that peace was secured for a long time to come. Hitler had realised every aim justifiable by reference to the national right of self-determination which, at least theoretically, had been considered a fundamental principle of the

European order ever since the peace treaties. He had stated explicitly that after solving the Sudeten German question Germany had no more territorial demands in Europe. "The moment the Czechs come to terms with their other minorities," he had declared, ". . . I will no longer be interested in the Czech state. And I will guarantee that! We haven't the least desire for any Czechs!" (Speech on September 26th 1938.)

But Hitler made no guarantee of the new Czech frontiers. A few weeks later the peaceful illusions of Munich were destroyed. On October 9th, in a speech in Saarbruecken, he adopted an attitude towards Britain which was in flagrant contradiction of the spirit of the Anglo-German declaration of September 30th. A vain attempt to revive the spirit of Munich was made in a Franco-German agreement on December 6th. The agreement remained without effect. In France, as in Britain, the conviction became general that further German acts of aggression were only to be expected and that the order of the day must be extensive rearmament.

Hitler, in fact, was already preparing the next stroke. On October 21st 1938 he had already furnished the Wehrmacht with secret directives for "finishing off the remainder of Czechoslovakia". He was determined to take the next opportunity of seizing what had been denied him at Munich. His political preparations aimed at casting doubts on the good faith of Czechoslovakia towards Germany while creating tension and difficulties by playing off the Slovaks' desire for independence against the Czechs.

On March 14th 1939 Slovakia, under German pressure, declared her independence and so produced the crisis which

Hitler required. The Czechoslovak President, Hácha, made an urgent request for a meeting in Berlin. There he was forced by threats of military action to sign an agreement in which he declared that he "placed the fate of the Czech people in the hands of the Fuehrer of the German Reich". Even as the discussions were going on, German troops had crossed the Czechoslovak frontier for the march on Prague. On March 16th Hitler announced that the territory of the Czech State had become, as the "Protectorate of Bohemia and Moravia", a part of the Greater German Reich. Finally, on March 22nd, he forced Lithuania to hand back Memel.

Europe and the Polish Question

THE snatch at Prague was a fateful event. It proved the decisive turning-point in Hitler's career and unleashed developments leading directly to the war and eventually to the abyss. The agreement at Munich, to which the Western Powers had given their consent only on the tacit assumption that this was Hitler's last territorial demand and that he would keep the peace in future, was cynically torn up. The world at last realised that the revision of the Treaty of Versailles and Hitler's evocation of the right of self-determination were only pretexts for an imperialist policy of conquest. In Austria and the Sudetenland the Reich had acquired territories which were linguistically and ethnically German. In the "Protectorate of Bohemia and Moravia" it had for the first time, and contrary to all Nazi theories, annexed foreign nationalities.

The end of Czechoslovakia brought the danger zone of Nazi aggression closer towards Poland. Between Germany and Poland stood a problem dating from long before 1933: Danzig and the question of the Polish Corridor. A sensible revision of this unsatisfactory arrangement, with which the Polish need for free access to the sea had been satisfied at Versailles, was a German concern for which the Treaty Powers entertained a certain sympathy. But after Prague nobody could keep up the belief that Hitler was merely interested in sensible revisions. The reaction of the European Powers to the aggressive attitude which Hitler began to adopt towards Poland was marked by the conviction that Hitler's aim was not the revisions he demanded but the conquest of "living space" in the East.

Covered by the German-Polish Treaty of 1934, Hitler had left the Polish question undisturbed as long as he needed Poland's neutrality. After the annexation of Austria and Czechoslovakia he saw no further reason for consideration. Within a few weeks of Munich he informed Poland that the time had come to settle old issues. On October 24th 1938 Ribbentrop told Lipski, the Polish Ambassador in Berlin, that Germany wished to discuss a "general settlement" of all problems between the two countries. Germany demanded the return of Danzig and the construction of an extra-territorial traffic route through the Corridor. Warsaw rejected this first German advance out of hand. After the German occupation of Prague the German Foreign Minister renewed his Government's demands with greater urgency, and diplomatic discussions between Germany and Poland now turned upon these questions with increasing acrimony, with Poland clinging tenaciously to her original attitude.

The tension caused by Germany's demands and their consistent rejection by the Polish Government ceased to be a purely German-Polish problem. It resulted in the formation of broad political fronts which were to become, within a few months, war fronts.

On the opposing side Great Britain assumed political leadership. Prague had led to a radical renunciation of the policy of appeasement of which Munich had become the symbol. It was Chamberlain himself, the most ardent champion of appeasement, who made this change in British foreign policy. Ever since Prague, Britain had become convinced that Hitler was trying to eliminate her influence on the Continent in order to have a free hand in the East, and that he was seeking European hegemony. In March 1939 Britain tried to obtain a joint Anglo-French-Polish-Soviet guarantee for all European states whose independence might be threatened in the future. The attempt failed through Poland's eternal reluctance to collaborate with the Soviet Union. As a result, Britain gave Poland a unilateral guarantee at the end of March, to which Poland responded a few days later with a similar guarantee to Britain. By declaring her solidarity, France reactivated her old treaty of 1921 with Poland, which in the shadow of the German-Polish Treaty of 1934 had become politically ineffective. The British guarantee to Poland was followed in April by similar declarations to Rumania and Greece.

On April 28th Hitler countered the British initiative by abrogating the Anglo-German Naval Agreement of 1935 and the German-Polish Treaty of 1934, regardless of the fact that neither agreement permitted abrogation without notice. From now on, German propaganda accused Great Britain of pursuing a policy of encirclement, thereby awakening, in Germany, disquieting memories. At the same time, adopting the formulae used in the preparation of the Sudeten crisis the year before, it accused the Polish Government of terrorising its German minorities. In May Hitler managed to confirm the collaboration of the Berlin-Rome "axis" in a formal military alliance, which later, however, was to disappoint the expectations expressed by its official name, the "Pact of Steel". During these same weeks Denmark, Latvia and Estonia accepted German offers of non-aggression pacts. On the other side, England extended her promises of assistance to include Turkey.

Since the beginning of April the Wehrmacht had been in possession of directives for the event of a war with Poland. Preparations were to be accelerated so that it would be possible to commence operations "at any time from September 1st 1939 onwards". This did not mean that Hitler had decided to act, although he was to begin the war on exactly that date. Hitler realised that the Polish problem could no longer be treated in isolation—that upon it hung the whole peace of Europe. As in the case of Czechoslovakia, he was only going to march if he was certain of avoiding involvement in a war on two fronts. After the spring of 1939 his political efforts were therefore directed towards Poland's isolation. The Western Powers, on their side, were trying to weave Germany's eastern neighbours, particularly Poland and Rumania, into a comprehensive system of security pacts. As both sides pursued their diplomatic activities, the summer saw a dramatic race for the favour of the Soviet Union, on which each pinned its hopes of tipping the balance.

In March 1939 Britain and France had entered into *pourparlers* with Russia, since effective help to the smaller states of Eastern Europe seemed impossible without Russian participation. The Russians showed willingness. But there were difficulties in the way of formulating a joint plan. Britain wanted the Soviet Union merely to associate itself with the guarantees which she herself had given. Russia, on the other hand, suggested a Soviet-Anglo-French pact with much farther-reaching commitments. France was prepared to accept the Russian proposal. But Britain was against committing herself that far. For months proposals and counter-proposals passed to and fro. At last, on July 24th, a political pact was agreed upon which stipulated mutual assistance in the event of any of the three Powers being attacked, and which promised assistance to a number of smaller European states, including Poland and Rumania. England had gone thus far to meet Russian wishes at the anxious insistence of France. But the pact was a fiction, for it was only to come into force when agreement had been reached on a supplementary military convention. During the subsequent discussions, the military experts came up against the same difficulties which had beset the diplomats. The obstacle was the attitude of the smaller states. The Soviet Union demanded the right to march through Poland and Rumania, without which her military co-operation in defence against Nazi aggression was difficult to visualise. But both states refused to grant this right, fearing to compromise themselves irrevocably with Germany and at the same time to deliver themselves into the equally feared hands of the Soviet Union. Poland, in particular, considered her independence of the two (as she thought) irreconcilable Powers to be a positive political asset. Only under steady French pressure did she begin to show signs of cautious agreement. Just as the discussions seemed to be showing renewed promise, they were brought to a lamentable end by the sensational news of the German-Soviet non-aggression pact. Hitler had outstripped the Western Powers in equally long, but secret, discussions in Moscow.

97

G

The documents so far made public give no clear answer as to which side initiated the German-Soviet talks. After the spring of 1939 each seems to have had an inclination to put out feelers about the possibility of a German-Soviet understanding. The *rapprochement* proceeded slowly, in careful and suspicious diplomatic talks, which at first were concerned with economic relations, but were later extended by the Russians to include political questions. It was a sign of Russian seriousness that on May 5th 1939 the representative of Soviet collaboration with the West, Litvinov, was replaced as Foreign Minister by Molotov, the confidant of Stalin. Moscow did not fail to point out discreetly to Berlin the implications of this change. If the talks made no further progress until July, one reason was Germany's suspicion that Moscow merely intended to use her tractability as a means of exerting pressure in its treaty discussions with the West. But the slow progress of these discussions was to be the very reason why the German-Soviet talks quickly gathered substance from the end of July onwards. On August 12th, the same day that an Anglo-French Staff mission began talks in Moscow about the proposed military convention, the Russians intimated in Berlin that they were ready to open direct discussions on all questions of mutual interest, with Berlin as the suggested meeting-place. Suddenly all obstacles were removed on the German side too. Ribbentrop declared his willingness to come to Moscow and suggested an earlier date. After agreeing on the points to be discussed, Hitler sent a personal telegram to Stalin and so managed to get the date of Ribbentrop's visit advanced several days beyond that suggested by the Russians. Time was running short if he was to attack Poland this year.

On August 23rd Ribbentrop flew to Moscow and the same night signed a German-Soviet non-aggression pact with Molotov. But the most important result of the Berlin-Moscow understanding was contained in an additional secret protocol which defined each side's sphere of interest in Europe. In this secret agreement Germany declared her disinterest in Finland, Latvia, Estonia and Bessarabia. "In the event of a territorial and political transformation of the territories belonging to the Polish State," as the protocol so unequivocally put it, the interests of both sides were to be delimited approximately by the line of the Narev, Vistula and San.

For both countries the pact meant a complete reversal of their existing policies. For both it was in blatant contrast to their ideologies: to Nazi anti-Bolshevism as much as to Communist anti-Fascism. The cynicism with which both sides brushed aside ideological obstacles, and the ease with which their propaganda machines managed to bring round the mass of their followers, showed an underlying kinship. Neither Hitler nor Stalin can seriously have believed that the *entente* would last. For each it was a tactical move within the framework of his political ideas, whose final aims were directed implacably against the other party.

Hitler was so obsessed by his Polish plans that in order to avoid the danger of a two-front war—the only obstacle he took seriously—he was prepared to pay the enormous price of the Russian pact and give up vast sectors of the belt of small states which screened Central Europe from the Soviet Union. He was convinced that the Western Powers would sacrifice Poland, which in its position of a wedge between two big Powers was now militarily out of their reach. To gain temporary freedom of action, he played this short-sighted and frivolous game on a plane which was no longer merely German but European, a game which in the end made possible Russia's expansion to Central Germany.

The Russians seemed to have given much more serious thought to the conclusion of their pact with Hitler. Their official argument, that they merely wanted peace, is refuted by the Additional Protocol, which contained the draft for the partition of Poland. The truth is that by making the pact with Hitler, Stalin made the war possible. For a treaty between Russia and the Western Powers would have been the one means—at least at this stage—of preventing Hitler from setting the world alight. But faced with the alternative of a pact with the West or a pact with Hitler, Stalin chose the latter. Hitler had more to offer: a chance for the Soviet Union to extend its influence in the East European states which the Treaty of Versailles had established in Russia's absence as a anti-Soviet *cordon sanitaire*. The pact with the Western Powers would have obliged the Soviet Union to defend these states. If the Russians were convinced that Hitler would sooner or later make war on them, there was a good argument for gaining time and strategic outposts to the West, both of which were offered by the pact with Germany. For the rest, the Russians may have doubted if a treaty with the Western Powers would really mean effective protection against a German attack. Munich was an awkward memory. For there the Western Powers had ignored Russia and come to terms with Germany. After that, it did not seem so very far-fetched to suppose that Britain might one day come to another agreement with Hitler and grant him a free hand in the East. From the Communist point of view, the Western Powers and Fascist Germany belonged to the same world of capitalist imperialism and shared a common bond of anti-Communist solidarity. It was an old maxim of Communist ideology that the word revolution was furthered most effectively by inter-necine wars between the capitalist states. This was yet another prospect offered by the pact with Hitler.

When the news of the German–Soviet Pact broke on August 23rd it was a shock to the whole world. War now seemed inevitable, for Hitler no longer saw any obstacle in his way to attacking Poland. The feverish diplomatic activity in the European capitals during the last week of August was no longer capable of deflecting fate. As for Germany, she was mainly concerned to justify her own action and ensure that future debates on the question of guilt would be coloured by the Nazi viewpoint.

On August 22nd the British Government was already apprised of the imminent conclusion of the Moscow Pact. Chamberlain lost no time in assuring Hitler, by a letter on the same evening, that Britain would stand by her obligations to Poland under any circumstances. On August 25th Britain confirmed her attitude by signing a formal pact of assistance with Poland. The change of attitude which Hitler had hoped would result from his pact with Russia did not occur. But while London considered the implications of the pact quite calmly, France was thrown into some confusion. At first Daladier treated the news from Moscow as a journalistic hoax. There were still illusions in France about reaching a Western agreement with Moscow, and the defeatest question "Mourir pour Dantzig?" went the rounds of the country. In Poland the atmosphere was much quieter, for the nation's conceit at its own strength seemed to prevent it from realising that the German-Soviet agreement had put it in mortal danger. An unexpected and highly embarrassing development for Hitler was the reaction of Italy in face of the British stand: on the afternoon of August 25th Mussolini informed Hitler that Italy, unfortunately, was not ready for war.

Probably under the impact of this news, which reached Berlin simultaneously with the news of the signing of the Anglo-Polish Treaty, Hitler, on the evening of August 25th, revoked the order, given a few hours before, to attack Poland next morning. All at once he seems to have become unsure of himself, if only in the matter of timing. He wanted to gain time for discussion, in the hope that Britain would yet give in.

About noon on the same day he had already made a far-reaching political offer to Henderson, the British Ambassador in Berlin. He may only have intended to confuse London at the moment of the attack on Poland (which, at the time of the meeting with Henderson, was still planned for the next day) and to paralyse its ability to act. But at the same time it was once again an expression of his old dream of Anglo-German friendship. He offered to guarantee the British Empire and make Germany's resources available for its defence. Britain, in return, was to give him a free hand in Poland. London's answer was handed over by Henderson on the evening of August 28th. While making cautious advances regarding a future Anglo-German understanding, it declared a peaceful settlement of the German-Polish conflict to be an indispensable prerequisite, and that this settlement must be reached on the basis of negotiations between equals. It urgently recommended direct negotiations between Germany and Poland.

On the evening of August 29th Hitler gave his answer to the British Ambassador: he was prepared to take up the British suggestion of a German-Polish understanding and would expect a Polish representative with full plenary powers on August 30th. This was a thinly veiled ultimatum, formulated in the knowledge that it would be impossible for Poland to send a qualified representative in so short a time. Hitler had no desire for any such negotiations. Sure enough, Britain declared his demand to be unacceptable in this form. The memory of Hácha's visit to Berlin was still too vivid. During the night of August 30th–31st, Henderson handed a statement of his Government's point of view to the German Foreign Minister. In a scene which has become famous and which hardly has an equal in the history of diplomacy, Ribbentrop told the British Ambassador that further efforts for German-Polish negotiations would be pointless because no Polish representative had appeared. Ribbentrop read out a sixteen-point document containing relatively modest German demands on Poland which he claimed were to have been submitted to the Polish representative but which were now declared ineffective. Against all diplomatic usage, he refused to hand the Ambassador the text of this document.

With this the Anglo-German negotiations reached a stalemate. In the last week of August they had been several times crossed and supplemented by the unofficial Swedish intermediary Dahlerus, who used his connections with Goering to try to bring about an understanding between

London and Berlin in the mistaken belief that Hitler might still choose peace. In fact, Berlin had used him as a tool in an attempt to keep England out of a war on which Hitler had already decided.

Late in the afternoon of August 31st Lipski, the Polish Ambassador, appeared after all at the Wilhelmstrasse and said his Government had been notified by the British Government of the possibility of direct negotiations; the Polish Government was glad to accept the suggestion and would send a formal reply within a few hours. Since Lipski could produce no special authority for making immediate decisions, Ribbentrop terminated the conversation in a few minutes. Further talks were indeed pointless. Six hours earlier Hitler had given the final order for the attack on Poland, due to take place early next day. Even a last-minute attempt by Mussolini to arrange a conference of the Great Powers could no longer avert the disaster. When, on September 2nd, Mussolini received the British Government's condition that Hitler must first withdraw his troops from Poland, he did not even pass it on to Berlin. Hitler had made it plain that Italy's attempt at mediation was unwelcome.

In the early hours of September 1st, without declaration of war, Germany attacked Poland. Hitler had ordered the attack knowing that he was risking a world war, although he nourished to the last a hope that Britain would remain neutral or at least passive. On September 3rd, Britain and France, in accordance with their treaty obligations to Poland, declared war on Germany.

1939–45
THE SECOND WORLD WAR

The Victorious Campaigns (1939–41)

THE German people accepted the outbreak of the war as an unavoidable disaster. Nowhere in Germany did the news of the German attack on Poland release anything like the patriotic exultation of the first days of August 1914. It was only the unexpected victories of the first few weeks which transformed the fatalism of the German public into the confident false optimism which thenceforward prevailed continuously until the first serious crisis at the end of 1941.

The German attack was launched with two Army Groups, from the south and the west and north west, in the direction of Warsaw. In spite of Poland's desperate appeals for help, the Western Powers made no attempt to invade Germany's inadequately defended western frontier. So Hitler was able to conduct his Blitzkrieg with the precision of a war game. Within a few weeks Poland was reduced to military and political collapse. On September 17th, when the outcome of the fighting was no longer in doubt, Soviet troops began to occupy Eastern Poland. On September 28th Germany and Russia agreed on the country's partition, altering the secret additional protocol so that Germany left Lithuania to Russia in exchange for Lublin and the line of the Bug. Danzig, West Prussia and the Wartheland were joined to the Reich. A truncated Polish state, centred on Cracow, was placed under a German governor-general.

Russia, likewise, began at once to consolidate her newly won positions in the West. From the Baltic states she demanded the right to military bases. Similar demands, some of them involving a transfer of territory, were made to Finland. Finland refused, although Germany did not support her. This led, at the end of November 1939, to the Finnish-Russian winter war, in which the Finns for a long time held their own against superior Russian forces. Before measures of assistance set on foot by America and the Western Powers in the spring of 1940 could become effective, Russia agreed to met Finnish peace feelers and on March 12th 1940 signed the Moscow Treaty in which Finland fulfilled her demands.

After the Polish campaign Hitler made a peace offer to the Western Powers which was based on his old idea of Germany's renouncing all ambitions in the West in exchange for a free hand in the East. Britain and France refused without hesitation. Hitler thereupon ordered the acceleration of preparations for a German offensive in the West. Against all the objections of his military advisers he wanted to open the attack even before winter set in. But the state of the weather forced him to make several postponements. Finally he decided to wait until the spring of 1940.

Meanwhile the preparations of the Western Powers to aid Finland against Russia by sending help through northern Scandinavia had increased the danger of their occupying Norway and so cutting off Germany from her Swedish ore supplies. Hitler had to postpone the offensive in the West once again. He decided to anticipate the Allied landing in Norway by a surprise landing of his own. On April 9th, a day after England had started mining Norwegian coastal waters in preparation for her landing, he opened the German attack on Denmark and Norway. Denmark capitulated without a fight. The Norwegians put up a bitter struggle, but in spite of Allied aid could sustain it for only a few weeks. In the end Germany won supremacy in the particularly hard fighting which continued round Narvik. Her losses were heavy, particularly in ships. While the King and the legal Government left the country, she set up a satellite régime under the Norwegian, Quisling, whose name was to become a byword for all who collaborated with Hitler in occupied countries.

The attack in the West began on May 10th 1940. Two German Army Groups crossed the Dutch, Belgian and Luxembourg frontiers. A third Army Group, stationed to the south along the Maginot Line, held back. Against the advice of the OKW, which wished to follow Schlieffen's idea and put the emphasis of the German attack on the right wing, i.e. the northern Army Group operating from the Dutch and North Belgian frontier, Hitler had adopted a plan of General von Manstein for a main thrust through Southern Belgium and Luxembourg and across the Meuse and Somme to the Channel coast. This plan, which in presupposing the violation of Dutch, Belgian and Luxembourg neutrality was no different from the alternative plan of the OKW, led quickly to a decisive success. Within five days the Dutch Army capitulated. Within eighteen, King Leopold signed the capitulation of the Belgian Army, against the protest of his Government, which left the country to carry on its resistance from London. Queen Wilhelmina and the Government of the Netherlands also fled to London.

The centre Army Group reached the Atlantic coast at the Somme estuary on May 20th, then wheeled north and by May 24th was in front of Calais. The main mass of the French Army and the whole of the British Expeditionary Force of ten divisions were encircled. Wishing to conserve his armour for future operations, Hitler halted the middle Army Group before Calais for two days. Thanks to this, the British gained time to secure a bridgehead at Dunkirk, which did not fall into German hands until June 24th. By then the greater part of the British Expeditionary Force and parts of the French Army, more than three hundred and fifty thousand men in all, had managed to escape to England, albeit by abandoning all their heavy equipment.

On June 5th the German offensive turned south and broke through the hastily improvised French front behind the Somme and Aisne. On June 14th Paris was occupied without resistance. On the same day the German southern Army Group opened the attack on the Maginot Line, and the German forces advancing from the French interior appeared simultaneously in the rear. Other forces pushed south across the Loire and south-west through Burgundy to the Swiss frontier.

France was in a desperate plight. The roads were blocked by endless streams of refugees which made all attempts to organise continued resistance impossible. The new Government formed by Marshal Pétain on June 17th turned a deaf ear to Britain's desperate calls to continue the fight, and asked for an armistice through Madrid. The armistice was signed on June 22nd at Compiègne, the scene of the armistice negotiations in 1918. It declared the whole of Northern and Central

France, including the Atlantic coast as far as the Spanish frontier, to be occupied territory. The French Army went into captivity in Germany. The French Government chose Vichy, in the unoccupied South, to be its capital.

The armistice could only come into force on June 25th, because France had first to conclude an armistice with Italy. On June 11th, when the outcome of the campaign had long been decided, Mussolini had declared war on France in order to be in time for the division of the spoils. Italy's ambitious demands (Savoy, the Riviera, Corsica, Tunisia and Algeria) made it even more difficult to pursue a policy of reconciliation towards France than Hitler had hoped. In vain did he try to win France into an alliance against England. Italy's entry into the war, which at first seemed to open new vistas in the Mediterranean, proved ultimately to be a heavy liability.

After his triumphant victory in France, Hitler was fêted by his admirers as the "greatest general of all time". He saw himself on the threshold of another victory, which he expected to decide the war: the victory over England. For a short while after Dunkirk he believed that Britain would be prepared to negotiate. But the British Government, headed since May 10th by Churchill, left no doubt that in spite of its desperate situation it had no thought of peace but would continue the struggle from the Dominions if necessary. So Hitler contemplated an invasion. Feverish preparations had been going on since July. But the immense difficulty of a large-scale landing now became clear, since the crossing of the Straits of Dover would have to be made without adequate cover from the fleet, which was outclassed by the undiminished power of the enemy's navy. Hitler hesitated. During the early

autumn it became obvious that the preparatory offensive oᴌ
the Luftwaffe was failing in its aim of achieving air superiority
over the British Isles. The defence of the United Kingdom
had not been materially weakened. German losses, on the
other hand, were high. After much hesitation Hitler decided
in the middle of October to postpone the invasion until
spring. But when the spring of 1941 arrived, Hitler was busy
with other plans.

When he cancelled the invasion operation in the autumn, he
was already considering a shift of the German war machine
in a very different direction—against his Russian allies.
Russia's attitude during the French campaign had confirmed
his belief that a military conflict with the Soviet Union was
sooner or later unavoidable. The latter had used his pre-
occupation in the West to improve its position *vis-à-vis*
Germany, occupying the Rumanian territories of Northern
Bukovina and Bessarabia and annexing the Baltic states of
Lithuania, Estonia and Latvia. Furthermore the dogged
resistance of Britain made Hitler suspect that she was encouraged by the thought that Russia, his ally of today, would
prove his enemy of tomorrow. So if England's defeat at this
stage was doubtful Hitler saw the elimination of the Soviet
Union as a chance to create a political situation which would
finally seal England's fate. After his triumphant campaigns
in Poland and France, he had no doubt that he could inflict
a crushing defeat on the Soviet Union within a few months.

His first orders for the Wehrmacht to prepare for the attack
on the Soviet Union had already been given at the end of
July 1940. For months the discussions about an attack on
Russia went on simultaneously with the planning of the

landing in England. The final decision seems to have been made in November 1940, at the time of Molotov's visit to Berlin, when the patent incompatibility of the two sides' political claims caused Soviet-German relations to start rapidly cooling off.

Hitler wanted to open the war against Russia in the spring of 1941. But developments in the Balkans interfered with his plan. In the autumn of 1940, regardless of the misgivings of his German allies, Mussolini had opened a campaign against Greece. This developed into a lamentable fiasco for Italy and was followed, in the spring of 1941, by the landing of British troops in Greece. If Hitler meant to attack Russia, he had to eliminate this dangerous threat to his flank and above all keep the vital Rumanian oilfields beyond the range of British bombers. Furthermore, at the end of March, there were unexpected difficulties with Yugoslavia, whose support in the coming struggle with Russia he thought he had acquired by an agreement. On April 6th Hitler attacked Yugoslavia and Greece. Yugoslavia capitulated after eleven days, Greece after fifteen; brilliant victories which increased his confidence of defeating Russia in a Blitzkrieg also.

On June 22nd 1941 Hitler attacked Russia, to the complete surprise of the German people and of the world. His pretext, that he had been forced to act because of Russian military preparations, deceived no one. Russia was certainly as cynical about the German-Soviet treaty as Hitler, but she had nothing to gain by attacking him at the height of his military power. Her hopes were based on Germany and Britain exhausting each other, and no doubt she was preparing to throw in her untapped power at the appropriate moment.

H

The campaign against Russia proved not to be the Blitz-krieg that Hitler had hoped for. After the first big victories, which cost the Russians terrible losses in men and material, the German attack, supported by Rumania, Hungary and Finland, was brought to a standstill before Leningrad and Moscow. A premature winter caused heavy casualties among troops whom a deluded High Command had sent into the battle without winter clothing. It was the turning-point of the war. Only a short campaign could have saved Hitler from his dreaded war on two fronts. Now he had to prepare for a prolonged struggle. There began an over-exertion of German strength, and with it the monstrous exploitation of the occupied countries in the service of the Nazi war lords. But the gradual decline could as little be stemmed as the irresistibly growing strength of a world of enemies. Time was on the other side.

The Enemy Hits Back

DURING the weeks when the German advance was becoming bogged down in Russia, the conflict developed into a world war through the entry of Japan and America. On December 7th 1941, after protracted discussions with America (who since the summer of 1941 had opposed Japanese expansion in China by economic sanctions) Japan attacked the American Pacific Fleet at Pearl Harbour, thus opening undeclared war on her. In accordance with their treaty obligations, Germany and Italy declared war on America on December 11th.

The treaty concerned was the Berlin Three-Power Pact, by which Germany and Italy had enlarged their anti-Comintern relationship with Japan into a political and military treaty on September 27th 1940. Hitler had signed it in the twofold hope that it would lead the Japanese to attack British positions in the Far East and that it would keep America out of the war, or at least immediately expose her to the handicap of a war on two fronts. One of his reasons for attacking Russia was a wish to eliminate the Soviet Union before America's entry into the war tied him down in the West again.

American policy had travelled a long way from isolationism just after the first world war to readiness to help Britain against Hitler in the second. In 1935–6 the dislike of Americans for any kind of involvement in European affairs had given birth to the strict Neutrality Acts which encouraged Hitler in his aggressive foreign policy. It was only President Roosevelt's passionate endeavours to mobilise opinion against the aggressor states and his calls for the solidarity of the democracies which slowly changed the attitude of the American public. When war broke out, there was no doubt on which side its sympathies lay. From the very first, within the limits of the Neutrality Acts, America put her economic power at the disposal of the Allies; as Germany went from success to success, and the Western Powers were faced with mounting difficulties, she discarded the Neutrality Acts and turned to immediate assistance of Germany's enemies. The material riches of the American continent began to be marshalled for war by a vast programme of rearmament. Through the Lend-Lease Act of March 11th 1941, Roosevelt began to supply Britain—and after the outbreak of the German-Russian war, Russia—with enormous quantities of equipment, raw materials and food. On August 14th 1941 he met Churchill on the Atlantic and together they issued the "Atlantic Charter", setting out the democracies' war aims. From this extensive political and economic engagement, it was but a small step to America's official entry into the war—a step which had so far been delayed by the hesitant attitude of American public opinion. Pearl Harbour forced this step, and at one stroke silenced every voice of isolationism.

Fresh German military successes obscured the fact that Hitler was already overtaxing Germany's resources and consuming them at a murderous rate. In the summer of 1942 he intended to force a decision in Russia by means of a new

offensive on the southern front. One thrust reached the Lower
Volga at Stalingrad; the other penetrated to the Caucasian
heights. In the same weeks the German Africa Corps, which
since 1941 had been stiffening the Italians in North Africa,
appeared under Rommel at the gateway of Egypt, El Alamein.
A bold pincer movement seemed to threaten the whole of the
Middle East. But the Axis had irrevocably passed the zenith
of its power. Supply over these thousands of miles could no
longer be managed. Rommel came to a standstill before El
Alamein, and in the autumn was forced to retreat before
Montgomery's successful counter-offensive. The troops which
had reached the Caucasus lacked the strength to push on to
the southern oilfields which were their objective. And
catastrophe was already on the way at Stalingrad. In spite of
terrible losses, the Red Army continued to appear with fresh
forces, and at the end of November it severed the Sixth
Army's communications by an attack from both north and
south. Against all reason Hitler refused to allow the army
commander, von Paulus, to retreat. In this way he sacrificed
some three hundred thousand men. Crowded into a small
space and dreadfully decimated, the forces under Paulus
finally capitulated on January 31st 1943.

Meanwhile the Americans had entered the war in Europe
by way of the Mediterranean theatre. To the complete surprise of the Axis, Anglo-American forces under Eisenhower
had landed in Morocco and Algiers on November 8th 1942.
Threatened from both west and east, the German-Italian
forces, whom Hitler had refused permission to withdraw in
time to Europe, could now merely try to hold on for a few

more months. Their capitulation in May 1943 brought the war in North Africa to an end.

In January 1943, after the German reverses in North Africa and Russia, Roosevelt met Churchill at Casablanca and carried his demand for the "unconditional surrender" of the Axis Powers. "Unconditional surrender" excluded a political solution of the conflict and decisively helped to prolong the war. It forced the German people into a despairing solidarity with the régime, whose claim that the enemy intended the annihilation not merely of Nazism but of Germany itself seemed thus to be confirmed.

From the security of their base in North Africa, the British and Americans launched their attack in the European theatre at the softest spot: they occupied Sicily and advanced across the Straits of Messina into Southern Italy. This had far-reaching political consequences. The numerous opponents of Axis policy—the Royal Family, the Army, and even some Fascist leaders—combined to bring about Mussolini's fall. On July 25th the Duce was forced to resign and was arrested. A new Government under Marshal Badoglio tried to preserve the same outward attitude to Germany, but secretly began to treat with the Allies. Hitler, however, forestalled the effects of a separate armistice, signed on September 3rd, by swiftly occupying Italy and disarming the Italian Army. Mussolini was liberated by a German *coup de main* and survived to be head, by the grace of Hitler, of a Fascist "Socialist Republic" confined to Northern Italy. In the further course of the war the German forces were slowly pushed out of Southern and Central Italy, but were able to prevent the Allies from entering the North Italian plain until the end.

As far as Germany was concerned, Italy remained a subsidiary theatre. The bulk of the German Army was tied down
in Russia, where it continued a desperate struggle with
immense losses. For the Soviet Union, Stalingrad was the
turning-point of the war. From then on, the Red Army
pushed relentlessly westward. It relieved Leningrad of its
land siege, forced back the German central front by hundreds
of miles, recaptured the Ukraine, and in the spring of 1944
reached the frontiers of Rumania, Czechoslovakia and
pre-1939 Poland.

Stalin achieved these successes without the help, for which
he had so often asked, of an invasion of Western Europe by
the Allies. It was not until the tripartite conference of Tcheran,
at the end of November 1943, that Roosevelt and Churchill
promised Stalin a "second front" in the early summer of
1944. The Americans decided that the offensive should be
launched against the French Channel coast. In vain did
Churchill suggest the Balkans, whence he hoped at the
same time to prevent Russia's advance into Central Europe.

The fear of a second front in France infected the German
High Command with a creeping paralysis. The building up of
a defensive front on the Atlantic drew off strength from the
already weakened forces in the East, and so helped the Russian
advance. When the British and Americans with their superior
forces began landing in Normandy in the early hours of June
6th 1944, Germany's position was already hopeless.

Persecution

BY cutting off Germany from the outer world the war created conditions ideally suited to the development of certain tendencies within the Nazi State. There was no longer need to consider world opinion. A vast field for experiment was opened in which those in power could plan and act to their hearts' content. At the height of the war this field embraced nearly the whole of the European continent. The Nazi régime looked forward to the complete subjugation of Europe after the war. This became somewhat more apparent in the occupied countries than in Germany, where the Nazis still practised a kind of restraint so as not to jeopardise the nation's war effort. For instance, Hitler held back on the Church question, although he was as determined as ever to do away with the Churches in the end. For similar reasons the régime was at special pains to camouflage the activities of those of its departments where violence and murder had been developed into a hideous technique, only allowing the leakage of whatever suspicion seemed necessary to sustain terror.

After the outbreak of war, and particularly when the military situation became critical, the SS rapidly increased its hegemony. In contrast to the mass organisations of the Party, Himmler, with his woolly biological ideas, wanted to make the SS into a "racial" *élite* of master men. Combined with this, he and Heydrich had a second object: to amalgamate the SS with the various police forces in a State Security Corps. Heydrich, who was as intelligent as he was unscrupulous, had in 1939 created the Reichssicherheitshauptampt or Reich Security Central Office (RSHA), a body which covered Germany and the occupied countries with a network of subsidiary organs of direction and control. Between 1943 and 1945 the Gestapo alone had a strength of more than forty thousand. There were constant enlargements of the Waffen (military) SS. Originally Hitler had meant to capture the last remaining bastion of the middle classes, the Army and its officer corps, by introducing a younger generation with Nazi training. As time went on he developed a preference for the alternative: the creation of the Waffen-SS as a Wehrmacht of his own. By the end of the war this numbered some nine hundred thousand men and there could be no doubt that it was the Waffen-SS which was to provide the standing army after victory. An official pretext was hardly necessary when in 1943 Himmler replaced the "bureaucrat" Frick and became in name what he had long been in fact—Minister of the Interior; nor again when, after July 20th 1944, he took command of the Ersatz (Reserve) Army.

Since the days of the unofficial concentration camps set up as part of the unco-ordinated SA terror in 1933-4, the SS had long perfected in their camps a system for the moral and physical annihilation of their political enemies. It was not just that the war extended this system to the occupied countries. "It necessarily led," as a secret order from the Ministry of the Interior put it on October 4th 1939, "to a substantial increase in arrest work by the State Police departments". On January 2nd 1941 the concentration camps were divided into three classes "according to the personality of the prisoner and the degree of his danger to the State". According to this division there should have been carefully differentiated camps for (1) "minor offenders positively capable of reform", (2) "more serious offenders nevertheless possibly susceptible to reform and education", and (3) "serious offenders almost beyond hope of reform". The last group had reserved for it the Mauthausen camp, whose "books of the dead" tell us all we need to know. But in fact the division was seldom adhered to, particularly in the fast-growing "branch camps". During the war the purpose of the concentration camps changed. The inmates were set to work in private industry or in mammoth works constructed and owned by the SS, and this brought occasional, very relative, "improvements" in living conditions. All the more horrible then was the effect of Germany's military reverses on these victims of Nazi persecution.

It was a custom of the Nazi régime during the war to make concentration-camp inmates available for top secret "medical" experiments "gladly and as a matter of course". Hitler and Himmler justified this action as necessary for the "public good"; it was only right, in view of the heavy burden which the German people had to bear in war, that "death-deserving" criminals and "vermin" should make their contribution too. Himmler threatened anyone who opposed the human experiments with indictment for high treason and used the special position of his SS to give active encouragement to the breaking of new ground and departing from "tired bourgeois principles". The heinous climax came with the murder of more than a hundred prisoners to furnish the "Ancestral Heritage" foundation in Strasbourg with skeletons. The object was to provide "science" with Jewish skulls.

A further scheme was the so-called "euthanasia programme". Hitler had long looked forward to carrying this out "more smoothly" in wartime, without "resistance . . . from the Churches". At the end of October 1939 he signed a secret decree, back-dated to the outbreak of war in September. It laid down that "the authority of medical practitioners, to be appointed by name, will be extended, so that those adjudged incurably sick by the most critical standards within the limits of human knowledge may be granted a merciful demise". The questionnaire sent out from the Fuehrer's Chancellery showed the real nature of the decree. For the chief criteria for "granting a merciful demise" were the individual's working efficiency and his race. In practical terms, the biological programme for weeding out "worthless life" came down to the elimination of useless eaters, with the subsidiary advantage of releasing beds, nursing staff, etc., for military purposes. According to their own count, the Nazis had gassed or otherwise killed 70,273 mental patients in special institutions by August 1941. Their relatives were deliberately deceived. The calculation did not overlook the saving to the State: exactly 885,439,800 Reichsmarks. When the painstaking camouflage was broken by gross negligence in the selection and dispatch of patients, conspicuous obituary notices, legal complications with trustees and even charges of homicide, there was widespread agitation. Prominent Churchmen were outspoken in their protests, in spite of the threat to their personal safety. Even the Reich

Ministry of Justice intervened. Since even in wartime Hitler dared not acknowledge his action by a law, he retreated a step and gave a verbal order in August 1941 for the temporary suspension of the programme. But it was continued nevertheless, particularly among mentally defective children. It was further put into practice among healthy children of Jewish or half-Jewish descent and finally among mentally sick prisoners, mainly Jewish, in concentration camps. Meanwhile the assistants of the euthanasia programme were earmarked for a task of yet more frightful dimensions.

As early as January 30th 1939 Hitler had "prophesied" that one result of a new world war (blamed in advance on "international Jewish capitalism") would be the extermination of the Jewish race in Europe. When certain SS formations committed terrible atrocities against Jews during the Polish campaign, a number of Army commanders tried to stop them. But as their resistance received no support from above, Hitler could easily frustrate it, show the recalcitrant ones his displeasure, and deprive the Wehrmacht of any share in the occupied country's administration—all of which was fraught with grave consequences. While Hitler began methodically to eliminate leaders of Polish national life, Heydrich herded the Polish Jews into ghettoes in the larger towns, whence they were later due to be deported and placed with the German Jews in a reservation near Lublin. But after the conquest of France an earlier plan was revived. The island of Madagascar was to become a German mandate under the French peace treaty and was to receive four million Jews under a police governor appointed by Himmler. These Jews were to be used "as pledges for the future good behaviour

of their co-racialists in America" and were also to be turned
to account as propaganda for German "magnanimity" in
virtually granting the Jews their own administration. The
project, "enthusiastically approved by the State Security
Office" and "prepared down to the last detail" was "outstripped by political developments". Meanwhile, in Germany
and the occupied countries alike, the Jews were deprived of
their last means of existence by an unending series of pro-
hibitions. They were stigmatised with the yellow star, forced
to work for the war effort and deprived of all legal protection. Further, they were placed under the jurisdiction of
the police.

With his plan to attack Russia Hitler combined the idea of
exterminating its Jewish population as being the foremost
enemy of German rule. During the first months of this
extermination programme in Russia, he must also have
decided to exterminate all other Jews within the German
sphere of power. It was the "Final Solution of the Jewish
Problem". Once the Russian campaign had started, four
"action groups" under the Security Service (SD), the Gestapo
and the Criminal Police were given the task of rounding up
Jewish men, women and children by telling them that they
were to be resettled, and then shooting them. It is probable
that more than a million Jews fell victim to this action. There
is no doubt that, to begin with, the Wehrmacht was not fully
informed. After its unsuccessful resistance during the Polish
precedent, it was confined to administering the action groups
for rations and supplies, with orders to let them act "inde-
pendently and on their own responsibility". We know of a
number of instances in which field commanders made

protests or intervened against this activity. But in general the Wehrmacht was busy with its own problems and, being constantly threatened with the dictator's displeasure, turned a blind eye. A number of soldiers did, indeed, endorse the "stern but merited punishment of Jewish sub-humanity"; but a growing number became further estranged from the régime.

While the action against the Jews took its course in Russia, preparations were already under way for the quiet and methodical extermination which was to be symbolised by Auschwitz. Beginning in December 1941, the same staff which had been schooled in the euthanasia programme put to death about two million Jews, mostly Polish, at first in Chelmno, and then, from the spring and summer of 1942 onwards, in additional camps at Belzek, Sobibor, Treblinka and Maidanek. Once again, the orders came directly from the Fuehrer's Chancellery. In June 1941 Himmler, on Hitler's orders, had already directed the commandant of Auschwitz to construct the great gas chambers which were to set their impress on the whole action. As from the summer of 1942 a small and specially selected staff gassed something like another two million Jews, this time from Germany itself and Western and Southern Europe. Equipped with special powers, the head of the Gestapo Office of Jewish Affairs, Eichmann, and a number of his collaborators in the organisation named after him, set to work in the "friendly" or occupied countries to round up Jews and transport them to Auschwitz. The central direction of the whole enterprise was placed "regardless of geographical boundaries" in the hands of Heydrich, whom Goering had commissioned on July 31st 1941 to "work out a final solution of the Jewish question in the German sphere of influence in Europe". Heydrich's assassination (May 1942) may have intensified the extermination action, but it no more influenced Hitler's fundamental decision than did the entry of America into the war or the military reverses still to come. Heydrich had got as far as working out the principles and methods for the uniform execution of the crime and passing them on to the "competent" Ministries of the Third Reich. This was done on January 20th 1942 at a conference on the Wannsee, whose purpose is clearly demonstrated by the so-called Wannsee Protocol. For in spite of the highly developed jargon with which the régime camouflaged matters of this kind, it is obvious enough what the protocol meant when it said that there would be a "residue" of Jews who would not be "lost by natural decrease" when drafted to "labour operations in the East" and must therefore be "dealt with accordingly". On the strength of a preposterous theory, an illogical principle—but by logical methods employing every device of modern science—the Jews were exterminated simply because they lived. The great pains with which the Nazis camouflaged the Jewish extermination programme show how conscious they were that they had long exceeded what they dared admit, even to their own people.

The German Resistance

IT was inevitable that the actions of totalitarian despots should cause reactions which in some cases departed from normal standards. The methodical extermination of the Jews was merely the farthest-reaching result of an ideology whose adherents claimed unlimited privileges for the "strong", and who consequently planned, or achieved, the extermination of further "inferior" human groups. Hitler's twisted nationalism made a reality of Grillparzer's gloomy prophecy of a development "from humanity, through nationality, to bestiality". Under the maxim "Law is what serves the Nation" (its Master being the sole judge of what "serves" meant) sentences were arbitrarily passed or increased, the most fundamental rights violated, the ties of conscience denied, the idea of neighbourly love put to scorn—in short, the bases of Western civilisation destroyed. The twisted idea of a national state inevitably brought about its crisis. The reassessment and devaluation of all standards, which Hitler himself had brought about, could ultimately not exclude patriotism *per se*. His frivolous phrase about the "ridiculous fetters of so-called humanity" was answered by a return to elementary human values which was to cut across all differences of policy and programme and become a bond between the various resistance groups.

It was a road beset with conflict which brought the nation's

élite to the final step of active resistance, of violating their
formal loyalties and finally making an attempt on the life of
the Head of State. From the very first, and particularly since
the outbreak of war, the Nazi régime had mastered the art of
bringing the best elements of the nation into a conflict of
conscience about their duty to the increasingly imperilled
State. In the end, it was a feeling of responsibility towards
their country which provoked the moving spirits of the
resistance to action. The true interests of Germany were not in
contradiction to a feeling of responsibility towards Europe.
The cleansing of her own house was the moral and political
prerequisite of Germany's re-entry into the family of Christian
nations. More than this, there were some idealists who hoped
that the solidarity of the various national resistance groups,
transcending frontiers, would form a sound basis for a new
Europe. Nothing would be more unjust than for the historian
to use normal standards to judge, or even condemn, attitudes
and actions which sprang from a revolt of conscience against a
perverted State, and this in an historical situation without
parallel. Far from justifying their actions by ethical principles,
the best men of the resistance were conscious that their actions
lacked an "ultimate justice" and that they could only submit
them to the mercy of God.

The organisation of the totalitarian state and its skilful
manipulation of the masses, who were for the most part
religiously indifferent, ensured that there could be no single
resistance "movement", but only a variety of overlapping
groups. And in spite of the growing number of enemies of the
régime, the unity of action necessary for a successful rebellion
could not be realised because of the power of the police. Most

I

opponents found moral backing and a source of strength in the resistance of both Churches. But for all the Churches' courageous protests against racial delusion, euthanasia and the extermination of the Jews, it was not really their business to enter into the political struggle. As time went on, it became increasingly obvious that the only people who could hope to carry on the fight successfully were those who remained within the apparatus of the State or in touch with the occupants of key positions having access to the means of power. The opposition, which included members of the former parties, trade unionists, civil servants, Churchmen and prominent private individuals, began to focus its attention more and more on the Army.

There were numerous enemies of the régime in the Wehrmacht. But the officer corps, enlarged and rejuvenated by Hitler's rearmament programme, was no longer a closely knit unit. Its leaders believed that the tradition of military obedience left little scope for independent "responsible" action, even though passivity was tantamount to acquiescence in crime. Failure to pursue the bold objectives set by its Supreme Commander—which were in apparent accordance with every military virtue—would have been like surrendering a piece of one's own nature. Yet in the summer of 1938, precisely on the ground of professional responsibility, General Beck had called on the generals to revolt against Hitler's plans for war, seeing in the Wehrmacht the true guardian of the *res publica*. Beck's opposition was founded more on a deep moral conviction than on military and political considerations. He also planned a purge for the "restoration of law and order", though it was not yet directed immediately against Hitler. But his call for collective action by the generals came to nothing, because of the objections of Brauchitsch. The subsequent plan against Hitler himself, known in London and prepared with Brauchitsch's consent by his successor Halder, General von Witzleben, and the State Secretary of the Foreign Office von Weizsaecker and his friends, was not carried out. It was based on the assumption that Britain would adopt a firm attitude and accept the risk of war. But Chamberlain declined to base British policy on the uncertain potential of the German opposition; he preferred the way of greater "safety" through the compromise of Munich.

Hitler's political success, here and elsewhere, his change of policy towards Russia, his vacillation before the final unleashing of war, explain why in the eleven months after Munich the opposition did not act. But the depressing failure of the action prepared in 1938 affected the various resistance groups more than anything else.

Renewed approaches to Britain by individual members of the opposition brought no result. Plans after the outbreak of war were frustrated, like so many others in the days ahead, by mere chance. An opportunity was missed with the SS outrages in Poland. During the offensive in the West in 1940 the leadership of the Army remained sceptical and inactive. Further, the war saddled the opposition with a new responsibility—that of avoiding a new stab-in-the-back myth. What the situation demanded was the creation, through talks with the enemy, of a climate abroad favourable to action inside Germany. But each new extension of the war by Hitler's offensives and violations of neutrality threatened to cut the moral and political ground from under an opposition's feet, and to turn the enemy's war effort into a struggle to annihilate all Germans. Such were the reflections which determined Beck and his associates in the course of their talks with England, conducted during the winter of 1939-40 through Dr. Joseph Mueller in Rome. The talks were brought to an end by Hitler's Western offensive. The ensuing series of victories robbed the opposition of the psychological atmosphere needed for action. It took the Russian winter of 1941-2 to bring any large part of the community to their senses. The plan of Beck, Goerdeler and Hammerstein for a revolt in the spring of 1942 was frustrated by the departure of Witzleben and by circumstances beyond their control.

Slowly the various exponents and groups of the resistance began to emerge more clearly. If Beck—akin to the officers of the Prussian reform age more in his habits of thought than in his vitality—remained the "mind" of the opposition, then Dr. Goerdeler, the one-time Reich Commissioner for Price Control and Lord Mayor of Leipzig, became its "heart". For years he had been in contact with opponents of the régime both at home and abroad, and now, as the Chancellor designate of a future Government, he appealed to the consciences of the hesitating generals. In the last resort he acknowledged but one world frontier—that "between the decent and the indecent". In the face of the "great error" of materialism his "democracy of the Ten Commandments" demanded a return to the Christian-humanist traditions of justice and truth and the dignity of man, which was to be achieved by "utmost exertion of the forces of morality". Politics were to be humanised by decentralisation and federalisation. There was to be a reformed Reichstag and an Upper

House based on the Estates of the Realm, providing a "conservative system of counterbalances". Without being "reactionary" in the normally accepted sense, Goerdeler's idea of the future, for all its social awareness, was not without bourgeois features, particularly in the "liberalism" of his economic programme. In this he already differed from the Foreign Minister designate, von Hassell, an aristocrat and professional diplomat, but above all a man of European culture and international outlook, who suffered deep distress at the crimes committed in Germany's name. Much like von Trott zu Solz, he tried unremittingly to keep in touch with Britain and America in order to further the plan for a revolt by securing tolerable conditions for peace. Hassell and the Prussian Finance Minister, Popitz, an administrator and financial expert with "authoritarian" tendencies, leaned more towards the concept of a planned economy and state socialism. With the politically and socially radical wing of the opposition, the Socialists, Goerdeler had at least elementary human, Christian and cultural convictions in common. Mutual respect bound Beck and Goerdeler to the Vice-Chancellor designate, Wilhelm Leuschner, who tried to revive the cells of the trade union movement. Leuschner was a skilful organiser and mediator. With him and the highly gifted, dynamic Carlo Mierendorff, the deeply religious Theodor Haubach, and Adolf Reichwein, a new Socialist leadership arose which thought more in terms of the Nation than hitherto. After Mierendorff's death (in an air raid), the Minister of the Interior designate, Dr. Julius Leber, played an increasingly important part, particularly through his influence on Stauffenberg. The Socialist trade unions, helped by the Christian ones under

Jakob Kaiser, Bernhard Letterhaus, Nikolaus Gross and Otto Mueller, provided the opposition with a network of cells.

A spiritual and practical link between the middle class and Socialist groups was provided by Count Helmuth James Moltke's "Kreisau Circle", which was politically and socially "radical" in the best sense of the word. Moltke was a member of the OKW as adviser on international law. In his circle, men of widely differing backgrounds—aristocrats, Socialists, Catholics and Protestants—discussed not so much ways and means of getting rid of Hitler as the future rebuilding of Germany on a Christian and Socialist basis. Possessing what was probably the keenest sense of the dangerous effect of Nazi nihilism on men's minds, Moltke was in favour of letting the disastrous process run its course so that it might act as a purge. He believed that what had happened in Germany was a "sin", that "the idea of man must be restored in the hearts of our fellow citizens", and that "the divine order" should become "the ruling standard in relations between men and nations". The Kreisau Circle demanded decentralisation of the State; efficient competition in industry; the dissolution of monopolies and the nationalisation of basic industries; self-administration as far as possible in the factories; and a growing participation of the workers in organisation and profits. In this, and also in the more constructive form of Moltke's draft for a constitution, the circle consciously parted company with Goerdeler, whose position was furthermore somewhat reduced through the growing importance of Stauffenberg and the Socialists.

The role of practical mediator between the different groups, that of general secretary and clearing-house, so to speak, was fulfilled by the circle of military counter-intelligence officers under Admiral Canaris and General Oster. As an "intellectual", the highly educated and elusive Canaris was ordained by fate to be an enemy of Hitler and his power politics. He protested to Keitel against the illegal treatment and sorting out (i.e. shooting) of certain categories of Russian prisoners of war, which, like the rest of Hitler's policy in the East, "assisted the mobilisation of all Russia's internal counter-forces to a general state of hostility". At an early stage Canaris became pessimistic, and on the whole tended to be less and less active in the resistance, preferring to let others act while he served as their screen. This was particularly useful to his Chief of Staff, Oster, who acted on his own initiative. The latter, a royalist officer of the first world war, had come to accept the ultimate step of "objective high treason"—for patriotic reasons and against the destroyer of his country—aware of the ethical twilight which surrounded all responsible action.

Close to Oster's circle, and basing his stand on theology, was the Protestant pastor Dietrich Bonhoeffer—whose approximate counterpart among the Catholics was the Jesuit priest Alfred Delp. In vain did Bonhoeffer try, through the intermediacy of foreign Church leaders, to get a pledge from the Allies that their attitude to a non-Hitlerite Germany would be different. In a summing-up at the turn of the year 1942-3 he put the truth succinctly when he wrote that "the great masquerade of Evil" appearing "in so many honourable and seductive guises" had confused all traditional ethical conceptions. "The safe road of duty", of obedience to orders, appeared to the German individual as a way out of the disconcerting abundance of possible decisions. But in fact it meant that he was satisfied with "a safe conscience instead of a clear one", and ultimately that his readiness to serve the community was misused for evil. The power of evil could not be fought with the simplicity of a principle; only the "risk of an action undertaken on one's own responsibility" could "strike at the heart of the evil and overcome it".

This action "on one's own responsibility" was undertaken by the disabled thirty-five-year-old staff officer, Colonel Claus Count Schenk zu Stauffenberg. His lively and unaffected personality had made itself felt in whatever circumstances he found himself: he emerged as the natural leader of that younger group of senior officers who began to appear in the "military resistance" from about 1942, particularly after Stalingrad. If he had at one time seen something to admire in the apparent vitality of Hitler's movement, his sensitive, frank and lively character was inevitably opposed to a régime which, instead of developing organically, turned a living political body into a soulless, rigid power apparatus. Stauffenberg had numerous connections with most of the non-military resistance leaders, and would apparently have preferred the Socialist, Leber, to be Chancellor designate rather than Goerdeler. But although he was connected with the Kreisau Circle through his cousin, Peter Count Yorck von Wartenburg, he cannot be exclusively identified with any programme or group.

No one with his eyes open could have long remained in any doubt that in spite of the cost in life and wealth, Hitler intended to continue the hopeless struggle until Germany was annihilated. Any thought of resigning the leadership in order to save the country was impossible for one who had identified the country with himself. The military oath of loyalty, which had once been taken to the Fatherland, was now taken to Hitler in person, following the seemingly meaningless but significant formula of his followers: "Adolf Hitler is Germany, Germany is Adolf Hitler!" Sworn before God, the oath at the same time made the swearer responsible to God for its observance. After many searchings of conscience, the young General von Tresckow—who with Fabian von Schlabrendorff had planned several earlier assassination attempts—declared that the unprecedented decision to assassinate the Head of State offered "the only means of saving the nation from the greatest catastrophe in its history". At the same time it was the only way to absolve the Wehrmacht from its fettering oath of obedience. On July 15th, even the régime's most popular general, Field-Marshal Rommel, demanded that Hitler "draw the proper conclusion" of the military situation without delay. Rommel had long found himself in fundamental opposition to the Fuehrer, and in connection with the revolt had decided with the Military Commander France, General von Stuelpnagel, to end the war in the West regardless of Hitler's wishes.

Certainly one might well have had doubts as to whether the removal of Hitler could still save Germany in the material sense, in view of the way things were going. An appeal to Roosevelt, stressing the desire of the German opposition to save Central Europe from falling "ideologically and physically" under Russian domination and pointing to the importance of freeing the German people from their commitment to Hitler if the democracies were not to lose the peace, had remained unanswered. Nevertheless, even without hope of securing better conditions for peace and "merely for the sake of the moral rehabilitation of Germany", the opposition was finally convinced that it must act (as the Scholls and Professor Huber* had done, in distributing leaflets at the university of Munich in 1943). Even if the attempted assassination should fail, "the practical object was no longer important". All that mattered was that the members of the German resistance should have "dared, at the risk of their lives, to take the ultimate step before the eyes of the world and history" instead of "lapsing inactively into shame and falling prey to paralysis and coercion". They acted without thought of glory, regardless of their possible misjudgment by posterity or the danger of creating a new legend of a stab in the back.

After various abortive starts, Stauffenberg, then Chief of Staff to the commander of the Ersatz (Reserve) Army, General Fromm, decided to carry out the attempt himself, using a time bomb. The attempt took place on July 20th 1944. The scene was the Fuehrer's headquarters near Rastenburg in East Prussia, where Stauffenberg was to report on the formation of the Volks Grenadier Divisions at the midday situation conference. It was not the removal of the conference to a wooden hut which saved Hitler's life, but the quantity of explosive, the shifting of Stauffenberg's briefcase and the thickness of the massive oak conference table. In the event, Hitler was only slightly wounded. Believing that Hitler was dead, Stauffenberg passed on the code-word to Berlin. But it was not until shortly before Stauffenberg arrived at the OKH headquarters in the Bendlerstrasse that General Olbricht set things in motion there, having meanwhile received reports

* See *Six Against Tyranny* by Inge Scholl, Murray, 1955

that the attempt had been a complete failure. What determined developments after that was not so much the action of Goebbels in persuading Major Remer (who had at first acted on the instructions of the conspirators) to change his mind, but rather the speed with which Hitler restored communications from the Rastenburg headquarters, the special radio bulletin announcing that the attempt had failed, the counter-orders telephoned by Keitel and Himmler to military headquarters throughout the Reich, the obedience to authority of the Army Signals Centre and a group of officers at the Bendlerstrasse under Colonel Herber, and, above all, the non-arrival of the force from the Doeberitz infantry school (intended to man the radio stations) due to the chance absence of their commanding officer, who was one of the initiates. In Paris, Stuelpnagel succeeded in bringing off his stroke against the SS, but although the Commander-in-Chief West, Field-Marshal von Kluge, was sympathetic to the plan, the latter shrank from creating a *fait accompli* by discontinuing hostilities at the front. In Berlin, the action was brought to an end soon after 2300 hours with the capture of the participants and their being shot out of hand by the now liberated General Fromm. Beck committed suicide.

Although Hitler at first blamed the assassination attempt on a "very small clique of ambitious, unscrupulous" officers, the special investigating commission of the Gestapo, four hundred strong, discovered other circles of opposition. The officers involved were dismissed from the Wehrmacht by a court-martial under Field-Marshal von Rundstedt; then, with the civilians, they were given a fake trial before the People's Court under Freisler, in which all were sentenced to death.

They endured untold suffering, torture and humiliation. A film was made of their execution so that Hitler might witness it for himself. Yet they went to their deaths in a way which bore witness once again to the moral forces which sustained them. Their enterprise as such had failed. The fact that the nine months following July 20th saw more people killed than in the whole period of the war hitherto was not the justification of their action before history. For the ultimate importance of that action was independent of success or failure. And in this sense their aim was achieved. Whatever the outcome, they set up a sign which showed those who survived them the way to spiritual renewal.

The Collapse

THE twentieth of July did more than unleash a wave of terror. It was used as a psychological occasion to demand further incredible exertions from the people. Goebbels became "Plenipotentiary for Total War Effort". Propaganda became even more intense and unscrupulous. Setbacks were blamed on sabotage by the opposition, while the further outlook was painted to look as rosy as possible by reference to apparently vast reserves of men and material and the development of "wonder weapons". The same picture was used to justify subsequent mass conscription for formations like the Volkssturm (Home Guard), which did damage to economic and cultural life out of all proportion to their military value.

If America's entry into the war had enabled the Allies, and particularly Russia, to go over to the offensive, Germany after the beginning of 1944 could be compared to a beleaguered fortress. The besiegers far surpassed the garrison in men and equipment. By July 29th the war was already lost. Systematic air raids on May 12th had struck at the synthetic fuel plants. The action was preceded by raids on the Rumanian oil-fields. From the second half of 1944, in spite of all counter-measures, such as the employment of foreign workers and the moving of factories to the East, production began to fall. The V-1 and V-2 rockets, launched against England from June

13th and September 9th respectively, were able to cause some damage, but could no more offset German deficiencies like the unsatisfactory production of jet planes and Walther-drive U-boats than could the far-distant prospect of a German atom bomb. If one asks why Hitler nevertheless continued the war, the first answer must be that he lived in the hope of a quarrel among Germany's enemies; he may also have set store by the development of new weapons. But the ultimate reason was surely that he could no longer dissociate himself from himself; that for him the only Germany which counted was the one which he saw personified in himself and his party. This explains why he could ultimately speak light-heartedly and contemptuously of the possible destruction of the German people which would leave only a residue of trash.

The last ten months of hostilities, from June 1944 to the end of April 1945, were one long act of retarding the end of the war, which cost the German people immeasurable losses in blood and resources.

Landing in Normandy on June 6th 1944, the British and Americans established small bridgeheads which could not be eliminated by the German troops locally available. Apart from the fact that Hitler expected the main Allied landing in the Pas de Calais and so kept back valuable forces, the German reserves could not come into action in time because of the enemy's superiority in the air. The enemy was thus able to extend his bridgeheads and slowly push back the German front. Germany's involvement in the West enabled the Russians to open their main offensive on June 23rd under the most favourable circumstances. In July they threw back the German line to Kovno, Minsk and Lemberg. The enemy in

Normandy had meanwhile emerged from their bridgehead and penetrated the Cotentin peninsula. On June 26th they had occupied Cherbourg (though the port itself was completely destroyed). The subsequent battles in Normandy forced the Germans to retreat step by step with very heavy losses. Because Hitler had ordered them to hold their positions at all costs, they were destroyed or crushed where they stood. Rundstedt and Rommel did nothing to conceal the result of these tactics from Hitler; and neither of them was in any doubt that the German front must shortly crack. When the forces in the Pas de Calais were released, it was too late. On July 30th the war of movement was initiated by the American First Army at Avranches. It broke through the German lines and advanced with surprising speed, some formations going westwards into Brittany, others going east and then north. As a result the mass of German armour was completely encircled near Falaise, and only a part of it was able to escape through a narrow bottleneck and so avoid the general annihilation. The following weeks saw the loss of nearly the whole of France.

In the East, meanwhile, the Russians had reached the Vistula and had crossed the Rumanian frontier in the south. Two days before General de Gaulle entered Paris at the head of the Free French and Americans (August 25th), a brief revolution had set up a pro-Soviet Government in Bucharest. This caused the German front in Rumania to collapse and placed all formations in the Balkans in great danger. In September German forces began to evacuate Greece. At the same time a new front was painstakingly established in the West. Starting from the Vosges and following the so-called

Western Wall, it abandoned Belgium in order to hold the southern frontier of Holland. In Italy the German front was stabilised north of Florence, where it remained, in spite of totally inadequate supplies, until the spring of 1945. But this was of no great importance to the overall situation. Even the successful frustration of a bold attempt by British parachute troops to penetrate the northern wing of the German Western front at Arnhem (September 17th) could not bring a turning-point. About this time the Russians succeeded in penetrating into Hungary across the Carpathians.

A lull on the Western front during October and November was obviously due to the fact that the enemy was improving his lines of communication. Nevertheless these autumn weeks saw the loss of the Saar and Alsace. The momentary stability of the Western front encouraged Hitler to believe that the enemy was exhausted and might be split in two by an offensive against his centre. He ordered the preparation of an offensive which was to start from the Ardennes and advance via the Meuse bend to Antwerp. Like all Hitler's strategy during these months, this enterprise, too, cast common sense to the winds. Thirty divisions were employed. They received fuel for only sixty miles. The offensive began on December 16th. It got no farther than forty miles and had to be written off as a failure after one week. The thirty divisions thus sacrificed were the last German reserves. From what was left of them, formations were built up and sent to fight the Russians in Hungary.

The battles of retreat during the last year of the war were classic examples of modern three-dimensional warfare. The Western Allies had complete mastery in the air and were largely able to paralyse German transport. The large and medium-sized towns of Germany were all but destroyed. The concept of an "open city" lost all meaning. The hard-working population was made homeless, and women and children had to be evacuated to the country. Thus not only was the war potential damaged, but at the same time the people were worn down by suffering and privation.

The new year began with a Russian offensive of great strength. On January 12th the Red Army broke through the German front at Baranow, south of Warsaw, and by the end of January had already occupied Upper Silesia. In the North it crossed the Vistula, cut off East Prussia and occupied Pomerania. In February Lower Silesia east of the Vistula fell into enemy hands. At the same time the enemy opened a new offensive in the West. There was no holding him. After crossing the Rhine, the Allied armies occupied Southern Germany, the Ruhr and Lower Saxony. At the beginning of May they had reached a line from Luebeck on the Elbe to Carlsbad, Budweis and Linz. Vienna had fallen on April 13th. On April 25th American and Russian troops met at Torgau. In a Berlin encircled by the Russians, Hitler spent the last days of his life in a world of unreality, playing with military possibilities which no longer existed. On April 30th he committed suicide. On May 2nd Berlin capitulated. With the independent capitulation of the army in Italy on the same day, there began a series of local surrenders which ended, five days later, in the capitulation of the entire Wehrmacht.

Everyone could see that Germany's enemies were principally united by the negative aim of destroying the Hitler régime. With the progressive occupation of German soil the day

K

approached on which they would have to adopt a positive common attitude towards the defeated country. Hence the conference which brought Roosevelt, Churchill and Stalin together, on Stalin's invitation, at Yalta (February 4th–11th). The outcome of the conference satisfied none of the participants; for the formulation of their points of agreement was open to various interpretations. The basis remained the demand of Casablanca, that Germany must surrender unconditionally. After this, the country was to be divided into four zones of occupation, and Berlin into four sectors. France was to be the fourth occupying Power, although General de Gaulle had not been invited to the conference. The northern part of East Prussia was to be ceded to Russia. Other, unspecified, parts of Eastern Germany were to go to Poland. In the first place, of course, Germany was to be completely disarmed, and the Reich was to be dissolved into a complex of smaller territories. Reparations, at a sum yet to be fixed, were also contemplated. Both Roosevelt and the American supreme commander, Eisenhower, were under the illusion that a reasonable compromise could be reached with the Russians.

With these few and somewhat hazy political objectives, the enemy occupied the whole of Germany. The occupation of the East was to prove totally different from that of the West. Admittedly the British, French and Americans let the population of their occupied zones feel the heavy hand of the victor. But the Red Army's occupation of the eastern zone brought results which surpassed the worst expectations of the population, and even of the Western world. Murder, rape and arson were claimed as the legitimate privileges of the victor.

The German inhabitants of the East took to the road to escape. The efforts of the Poles to clear the German population from the eastern provinces had the same effect. Flight and expulsion caused the exodus of millions—an exodus which would not have been thought possible in civilised Europe. It was a repetition, on a much more terrifying scale, of earlier examples: the Turkish expulsion of the Greeks from Asia Minor; Russia's resettlement of Poles, Lithuanians and Latvians; the activities of the Nazis in the German-occupied East. Beginning during the last months of the war, the stream of refugees grew to fearful dimensions and continued long after the capitulation.

As State Secretary von Weizsaecker had predicted, Hitler's war had led, after great early victories, to a German defeat which surpassed that of 1918 in every way. Hitler had rejected the opportunity, offered by Chamberlain's England, for Germany to satisfy her legitimate national, though not her imperialist, claims, and to become, as the strongest Power on the Continent, the eastern pillar of a four-power bloc directed against Bolshevist Russia. Instead, by his initial co-operation with Russia, he had destroyed the belt of states which screened Central Europe. His subsequent campaign against the Soviet Union, undertaken against all warnings, was intended, in Himmler's brazen words, to open a "free road to the East", make possible a Greater German Reich of "a hundred and twenty million" and "push forward Germany's ethnic boundaries by five hundred kilometres". But in fact, by his Eastern policies on the eve of the war, then by his attack on Russia, and finally by his short-sighted oppression of the Soviet people, Hitler had decisively helped to open the way for Bolshevism into the heart of Europe. Inside Germany a strong State was to have ended the quarrels of parties, confessions and classes by creating a "community of the people". This was to have resolved outdated conflicts on a new and higher plane, and to have created a living organism in which responsibility and privilege were put in just relationship according to service to the community. Instead, Hitler's totalitarian state had led, as the men of the Kreisau Circle put it, to the anarchy of a "power complex founded exclusively on technology". The coercion of the State had suffocated the free public spirit of its citizens. In place of a national common will there had arisen the irresponsible will of an individual who made himself judge of everything pertaining to the nation. To satisfy the claim of a dictator, every obligation of conscience and justice was denied, the dignity of man disregarded, and the beast in man set at large. After twelve years of Nazi government, the German people were faced with the question: would they ever be able to set up a State again?

INDEX OF NAMES

Index of Names

Alexander I, King of Yugoslavia, 63

Badoglio, Pietro, Italian Chief of Staff, 118

Barthou, Jean Louis, French Prime Minister, 62, 63

Beck, Ludwig, Chief of the General Staff, resigned August 1938 in protest against Hitler's Sudeten policy. Leading figure of the German resistance. Committed suicide July 20th 1944, 130, 132, 133, 139

Blomberg, Werner von, Commander in Chief of the Wehrmacht 1933-8, 14, 16, 49, 51, 72, 73, 74, 75, 76, 79

Bonhoeffer, Dietrich, Protestant theologian and member of the German resistance. Arrested 1943, executed April 1945, 135

Bonnet, Georges Etienne, French Foreign Minister, 87

Bose, Herbert von, Press officer to von Papen, murdered June 30th 1934, 53

Brauchitsch, Walther von, Commander in Chief of the German Army 1938-41, 75, 131

Bredow, Ferdinand von, German general, murdered June 30th 1934, 52

Canaris, Wilhelm, Chief of German Counter-Intelligence from 1935. Dismissed February 1944, arrested after July 20th, executed April 1945, 135

Chamberlain, Neville, 88 et sqq., 95, 101, 147

Churchill, Winston Spencer, 111, 116, 118, 119, 146

Dahlerus, Birger, Swedish unofficial intermediary, 103

Daladier, Edouard, French Prime Minister, 90, 101

Delp, Alfred, Jesuit priest. Member of the Kreisau Circle, arrested July 1944 and executed February 1945, 135

Dollfuss, Engelbert, Austrian Chancellor 1932-4, 77, 78

Ebert, Friedrich, German President 1919-25, 24